Tutankhamun – Reviving Egypt's Past for the Future

Theodor Abt

جمعية أصدقاء المقابر الملكية المصرية
Society of Friends of the Royal Tombs of Egypt
Gesellschaft der Freunde der ägyptischen Königsgräber
Société des Amis des Tombeaux Royaux d'Egypte

Tutankhamun – Reviving Egypt's Past for the Future

The Story of the Facsimile of the Tomb of Tutankhamun and the Meaning of the Pictures in its Burial Chamber

Theodor Abt

Living Human Heritage
2016

Living Human Heritage Publications
Münsterhof 16, 8001 Zurich, Switzerland
info@livinghumanheritage.org
www.livinghumanheritage.org

ISBN-13 978-3-9523880-9-9

LAYOUT: Merve Çakıroğlu and Theodor Abt

PRINTING AND BINDING:
MAS MATBAACILIK A.Ş.
Hamidiye Mahallesi Soğuksu Caddesi
No:3 34408 Kağıthane, İstanbul / Türkiye
T. +90 212 294 10 00 (pbx) F. +90 212 294 90 80
info@masmat.com.tr

Contents

Foreword

Until fairly recently, just before the Revolution, there were times in the Valley of the Kings, when, day by day, hundreds and hundreds of visitors wanted to see the Royal tombs of the Pharaohs. It was, above all, the tomb of Pharaoh Tutankhamun that was one of the main attractions. But the sweat and dust brought into this tomb by the many visitors created conservation problems for these unique testimonies of the past. Like all the other tombs, also this tomb had been carefully sealed off after the burial of the Pharaoh and thus was never conceived with visitors in mind.

The creation of an exact facsimile of the tomb of Tutankhamun is a veritable milestone in the preservation of these Royal tombs. This project was set in motion by the initiative of the Swiss-based *Society of Friends of the Royal Tombs of Egypt*. Happily, their activity could be combined not only with the excellent technical know-how but also with the financial support of *Factum Arte* and the *Foundation for Digital Conservation* in Madrid, Spain. In Egypt, the first tangible result of this cooperation is an exact replica of the tomb of Pharaoh Tutankhamun. It was presented to the people of Egypt in April 2012. It now stands on the West bank of Luxor, close to the Carter house.

As the original tomb has to be closed to visitors – first of all for restoration purposes, but also later on in order to preserve the original from gradually being destroyed – this facsimile tomb is a role-model and an excellent example of tourism on a sustainable basis.

We sincerely hope that this example will make it possible to create more facsimiles, first of all of those magnificent tombs of *Pharaoh Seti I* and of *Queen Nefertari*, tombs that have been closed to the public for many years. This work will take a few years. In this way, Egypt will be ready for the time, when visitors will hopefully return in greater numbers in order to see these wonders of the past. With these facsimiles no visitor to such tombs will have to have any bad feelings that his visit might add to the gradual destruction of these marvels.

Prof. Dr Mamdouh Eldamaty, Minister of Antiquities

18-11-2015

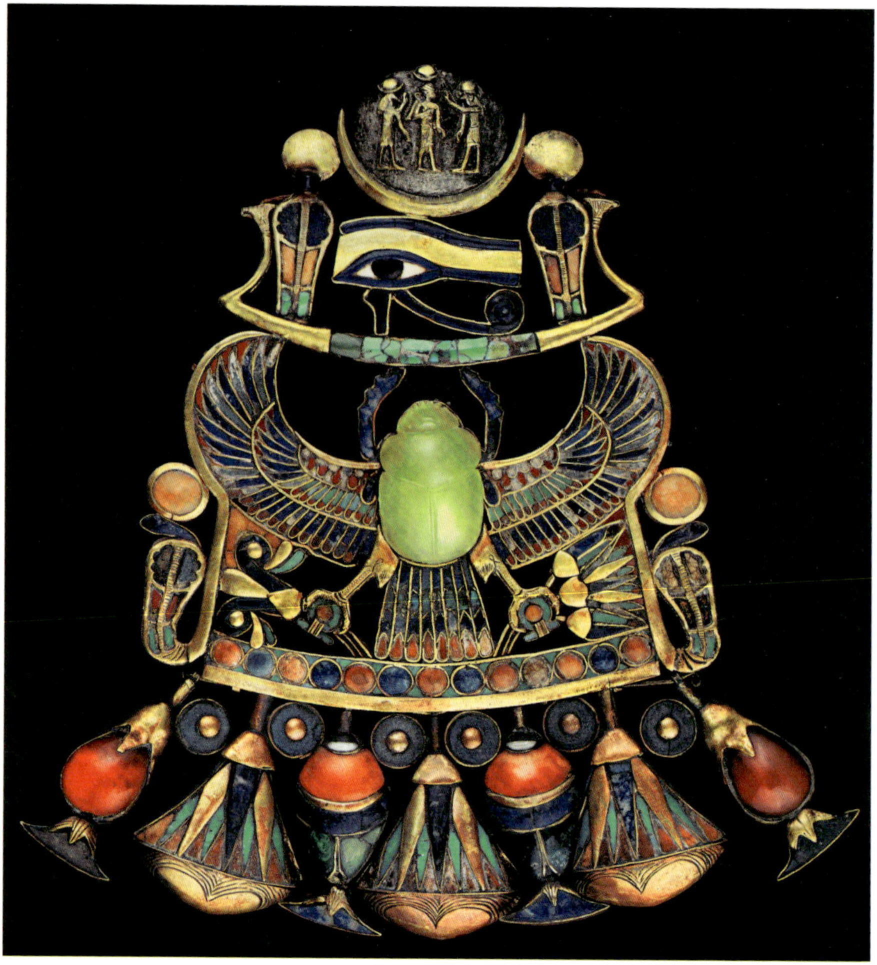

Fig. 1: Pectoral found in the tomb of Pharaoh Tutankhamun, epitomising the resurrection of the Sungod in the form of a scarab that brings forth the renewed eye, a renewal of the view that can see again that the light of the day (the sun), and the night (the moon), belong together.

Introduction

This book is intended as a guide for visitors to the facsimile of the tomb of Tutankhamun. **Part I** begins with an overview of what we owe to the Pharaonic culture in general. **Part II** goes on to the story of the rebuilding of the tomb of Tutankhamun. Then in **Part III** there follows an overview of the iconographic programme in the burial chamber. This section concludes with an introduction to the religious representations and texts, given on the four gilded shrines placed around the sarcophagus. These images and texts combine to provide unique guidelines to Pharaoh Tutankhamun in his tomb prior to his resurrection as Re-Osiris. The more we learn about the deeper meaning of these guidelines in the Pharaonic tombs, the more we can also see what all this may mean for us today. And the more these images and texts acquaint us with the wisdom of the ancient Egyptians about this world of the Beyond, the more we will be motivated to protect these treasures of the past in a sustainable way.

We are deeply grateful to Elhamy Elzayat, who founded the *Egyptian Sister Society* of the Society of Friends of the Royal Tombs of Egypt. Two distinguished members must be mentioned here: Prof. Dr Fayza Haykal and Prof. Dr Zahi Hawass both played key-roles in the realisation of this project. Our thanks also go to the Swiss Embassy in Cairo for continuous support since 1988 and to the Embassy of the European Union for its contribution. Most of all, we are grateful to the people of Factum Arte and its director Adam Lowe. They all not only believed in the urgent need to protect the Royal Tombs of Thebes, but also devoted their professional skills to this project and provided huge financial support.

For advise and for the reproduction of various pictures we are grateful to many contributors, first of all to Factum Arte in Madrid and the Griffith Institute, University of Oxford. Should this book be well received by the public, any profits will contribute to the creation of further facsimiles of Royal Tombs of Egypt.

Zurich, May 2015

Theodor Abt,
President of the Society of Friends
of the Royal Tombs of Egypt, Zurich

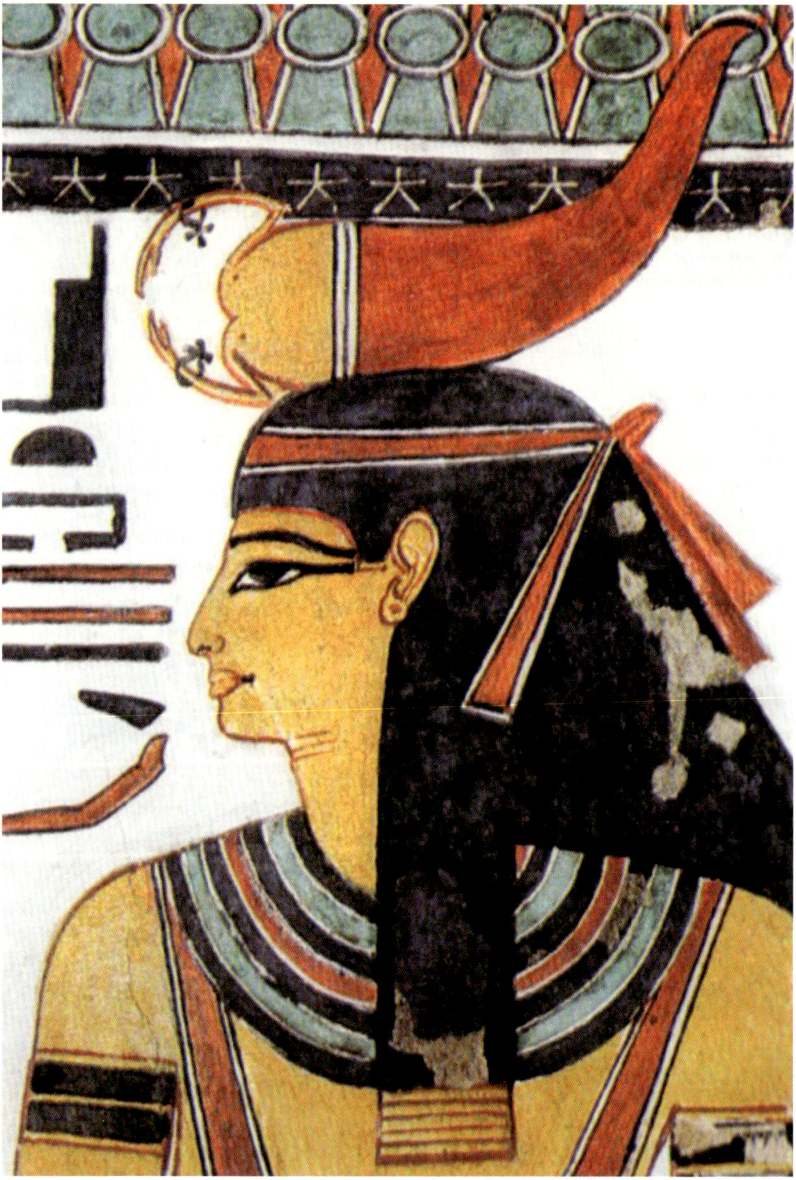

Fig. 2: The goddess Selkis from the tomb of Queen Nefertari.

Part I

What we owe to Pharaonic Egypt

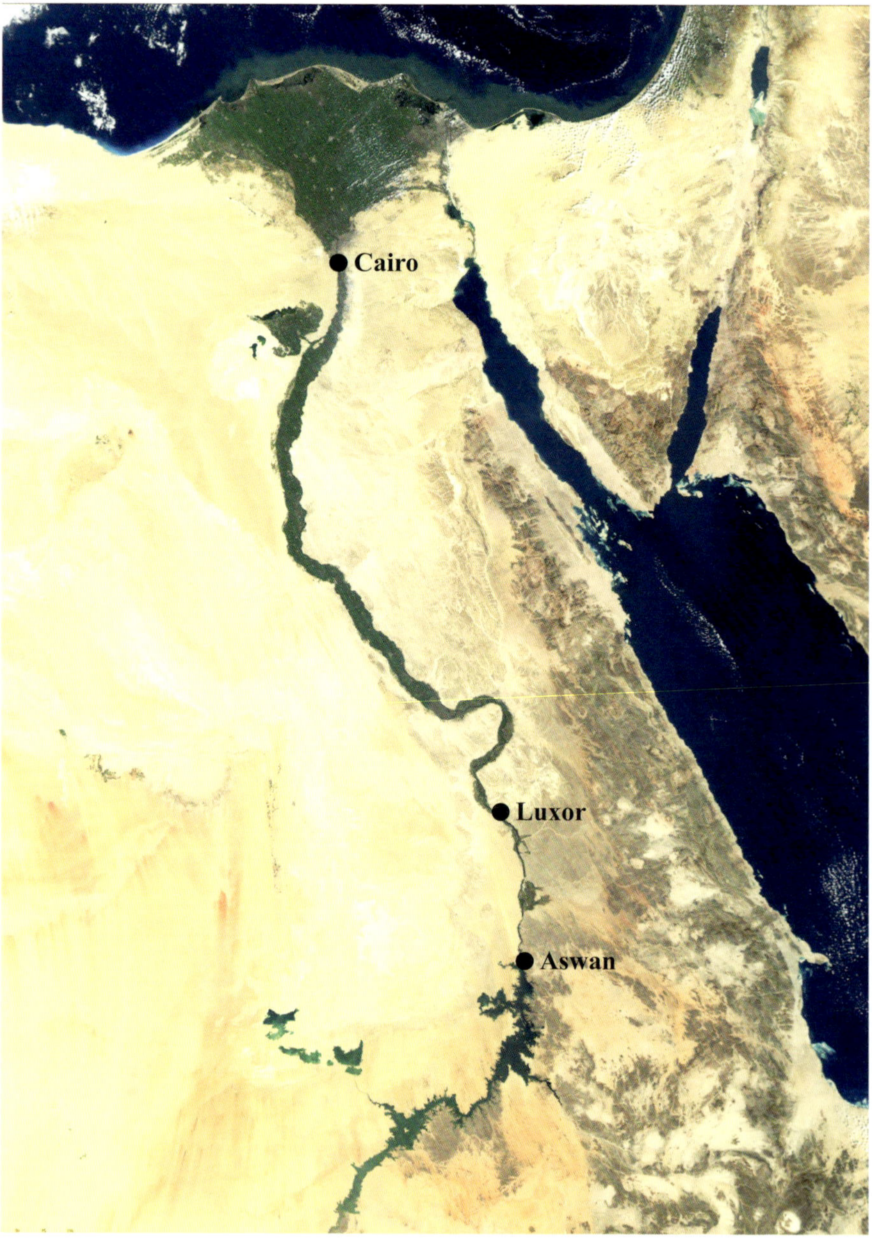

Fig. 3: Map of Egypt, «Egypt is the gift of the Nile».

1. Egypt – protected by Mother Nature

One of the fundamental aspects of Egyptian culture becomes evident when we look at its geographical location. On the picture to the left, we see a huge desert area south of the Mediterranean sea crossed by the river Nile, which provides Egypt's land with an abundant supply of water. Before the construction of the High Dam in Aswan, there were floods in Egypt every July. Then the Nile-water used to carry the needed fertiliser for the crops. This is why the Greek historian Herodotus was able to say: «Egypt is the gift of the Nile».

But the Nile is not the only thing that nature bestows on Egypt; it also shelters the fertile land along the Nile on all sides: the natural barrier to the north is the Mediterranean sea. To the east, it is the Red sea and the Sinai peninsula, to the west, it is the Libyan desert and to the South it is the Nubian desert and the Nile's first cataract at Aswan.

This natural protection allowed the ancient Egyptians to protect their rich crops and their wealth with the minimum of effort. This is a distinction which sets the Nile culture apart from other early superior civilizations such as those in Mesopotamia or the Indus Valley.

Instead of being mainly concerned with defending their wealth by means of a strong army, the ancient Egyptians were able to devote the surplus energy and time not required to produce food and shelter to pondering over basic questions of life. In this way they related *in a more introverted way to the spiritual dimension of life*, looking for answers to questions such as:

– Where do we come from and what is the meaning of human existence?

– What are the basic laws of nature, which must be the guiding principles for all humans?

– What are the major forces in human life, and how can they be influenced to become benevolent to human beings?

– What can we learn about the afterlife, and how do we need to prepare ourselves to greet this other world?

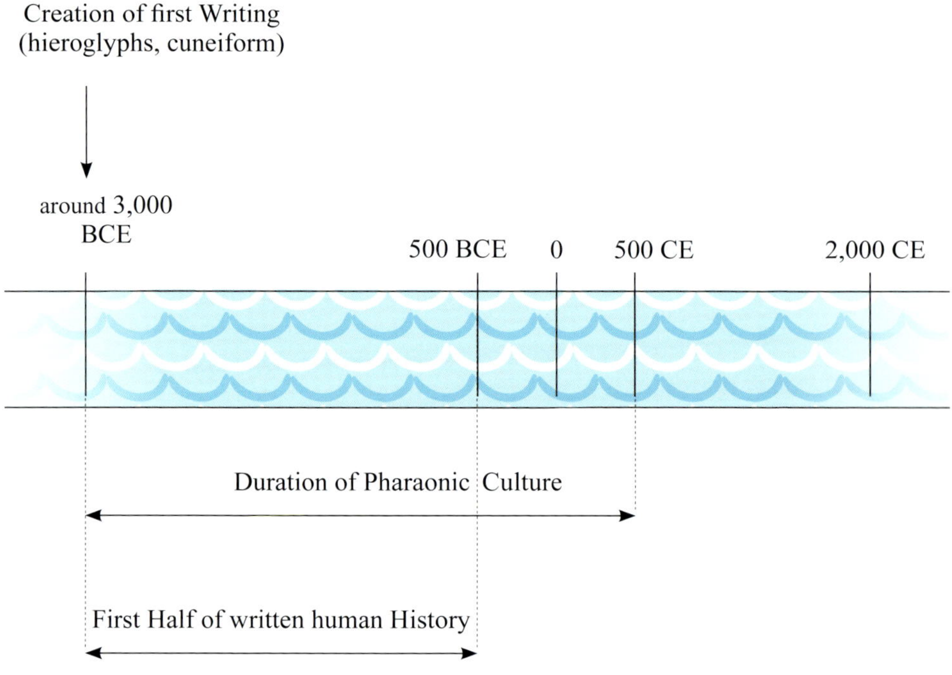

Fig. 4: The flow of time. The first half of human history was mainly written in Egypt, especially with regard to religious texts.

2. The first Half of human History – mainly written in Egypt

Why are so many people interested in – indeed fascinated by – Ancient Egypt? In our present civilisation, with its increasingly hectic and extraverted strides forward in material terms, we sense a *heightened longing to reconnect with basic questions in such matters as our human existence, its origins and its meaning*. These are questions that were fully acknowledged by Pharaonic Egypt, in that it was a civilisation that devoted enormous energy and love to pondering over these basic life questions, seeking to find a convincing answer.

Around 3,000 BCE hieroglyphic writing began to develop, at about the same time as the writing in cuneiform emerged in Mesopotamia. We can thus say that the written history of humanity came into being with Ancient Egypt and Mesopotamia.

However, the greatest part of the first historical records and by far most ancient religious texts known to mankind today originate in Ancient Egypt. As a result of Ancient Egypt's wealth of historical documentation, the study of its history, religion and civilisation now form a separate branch in the humanities: *Egyptology*.

Around 3,000 BCE, the first political unit was created on the banks of river Nile, forging together under one rule all parts of present-day Upper and Lower Egypt. This was the beginning of a 5,000-year continuity of Egyptian culture. *At that time a unique state came into existence: Egypt.*

Egypt is the only country in the world that – in spite of lengthy periods of occupation – has continued to exist as a nation over 5,000 years and is still an entity today. And Egypt remains a state that continues to play a central role, not only in the African and the Arab worlds, but also with the *Sheikh al-Azhar* – in the main part of the Islamic world. Egypt is known for its strong political influence and the stabilising effect it has in the Middle East.

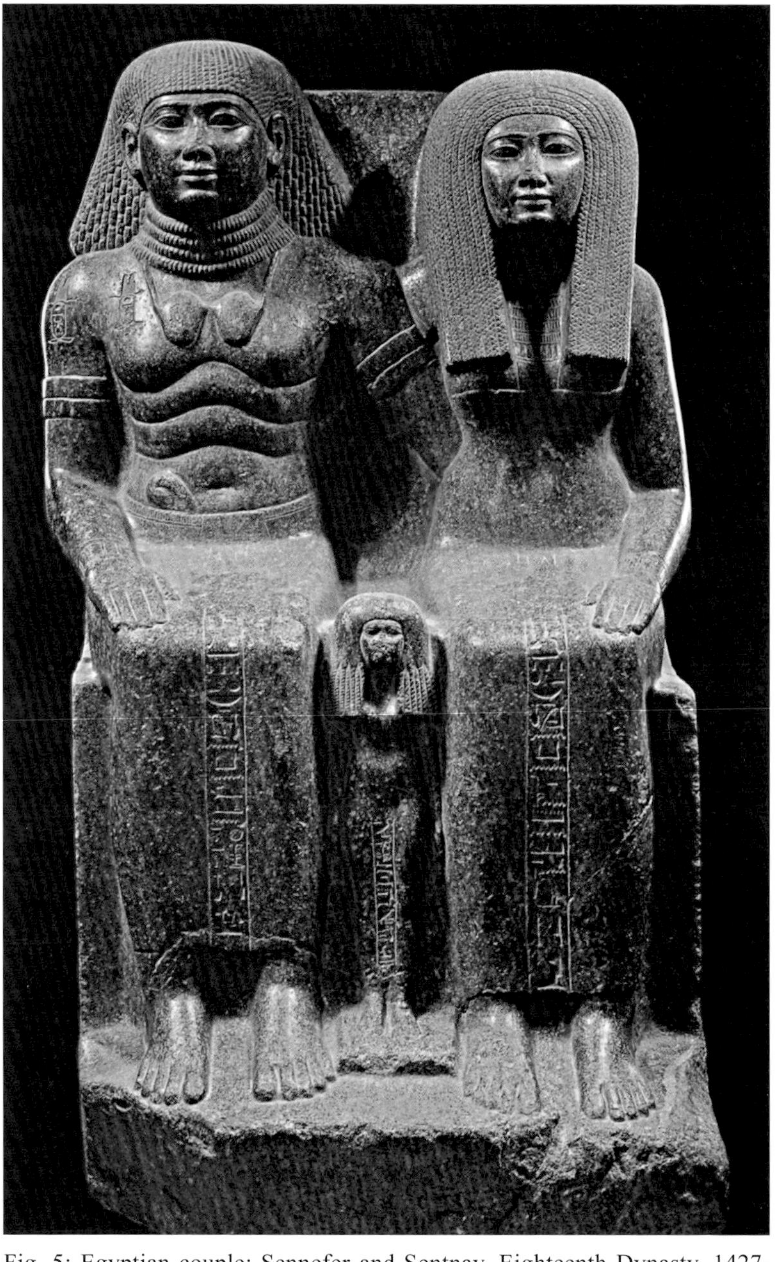

Fig. 5: Egyptian couple: Sennefer and Sentnay, Eighteenth Dynasty, 1427-1390 BCE, larger than life-size, granodiorite. The Egyptian Museum Cairo, CG 42126.

3. Equality of the male and the female Principle

As the first enduring form of higher civilisation, Pharaonic culture had a deep concern for its own constant renewal. The ancient Egyptians almost never disregarded the cultural achievements of their ancestors, but actually paid great heed to them. Such respect for the organic growth of culture derives from the insight that conscious cultural achievements cannot be maintained without constant acts of renewal. This effort and energy with regard to renewal is probably the reason why Pharaonic culture continued over a period of over three thousand years, mainly in peace, interrupted only by short periods of crisis and disorder.

To prevent and to overcome a crisis, basic renewal is called for. How was it possible that Pharaonic culture had the ability to renew itself again and again and hence endure for well over 3,000 years?

The key to biological renewal – to the birth of new life and hence to regeneration – is linked to motherhood and thus to the feminine in general. As the idea of rebirth was a key concern for ancient Egyptians, it is not surprising that Ancient Egypt had a *deep respect for the female principle*, and accordingly for women and for nature.

This feature can be seen, for instance, in the way both the Pharaoh and his wife, as well as ordinary couples, were depicted at that time: husband and wife were usually represented as being roughly the same size and with the same attention to detail. With regard to the respect for Mother Nature and her laws, we will deal with that in the next chapter.

The function of the female with regard to rebirth and renewal was fully recognized and played a central role, not only in the individual's quest for immortality but also in the renewal of society as a whole.

As we will see, the sky-goddess Nut and other goddesses played a central role in the sequence of pictures of the deceased Pharaoh Tutankhamun, protecting him and guiding him to his resurrection.

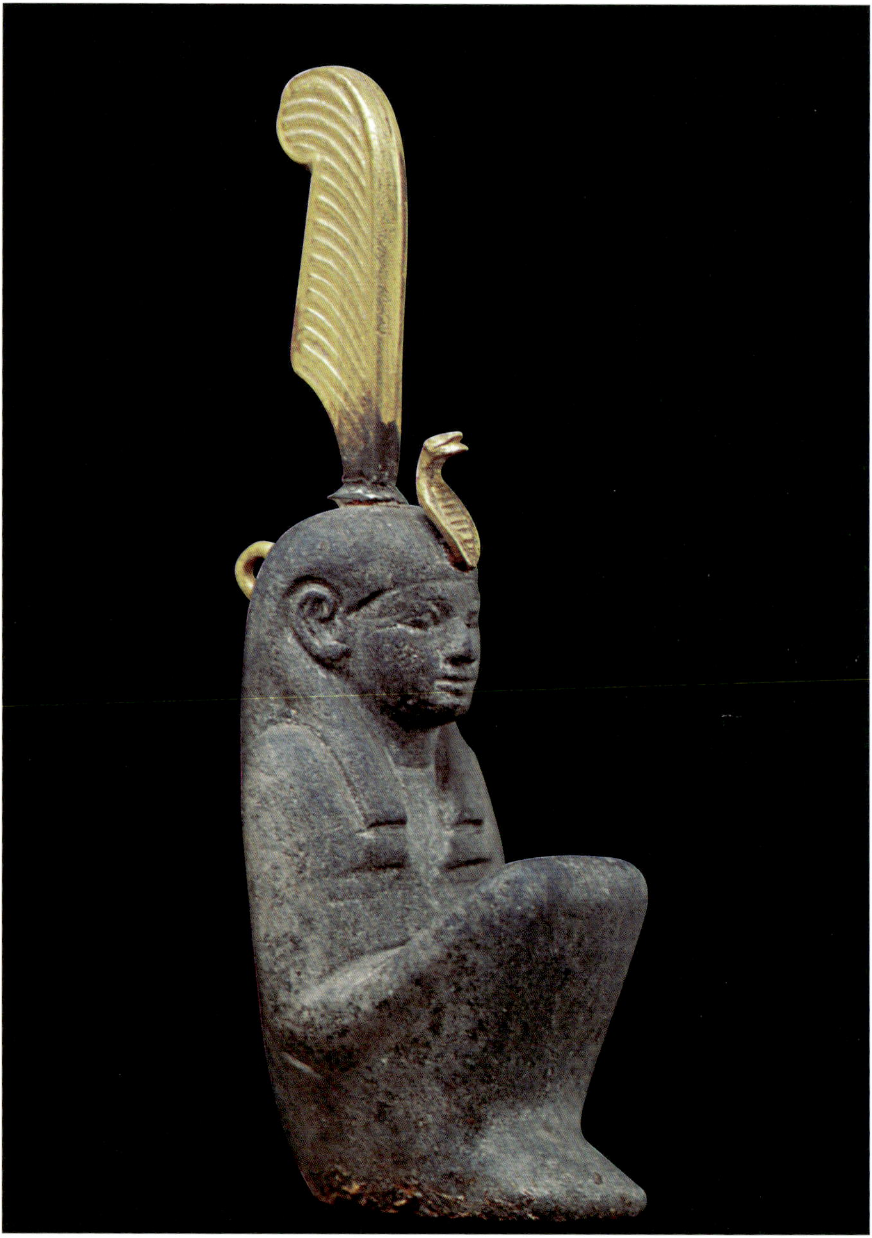

Fig. 6: Goddess Ma'at, Third Intermediate Period, c. 800-700 BCE, lapis lazuli and gold, height 7 cm. The Egyptian Museum Cairo, CG 38907.

4. The Pharaonic Concept of Sustainability – 3,000 Years of Success

When we look at the Pharaonic culture today, we cannot help wondering how it was possible for a civilisation to be able to *continue for over 3,000 years*, constantly renewing itself. What myth did the ancient Egyptians have which enabled them repeatedly to forestall and overcome social crises so successfully? The answer to this question, which concerns all human lives – especially today – is the Pharaonic concept of sustainability and renewal as well as the emphasis on a continuous relationship with the one and the many divinities in the Beyond, and hence their striving for an appropriate knowledge of the afterlife.

One of the most enduring and fascinating aspects of this Pharaonic culture is the idea of the *divine cosmic order, balance and justice, symbolised in the goddess Ma'at.* She was considered to counter-balance the permanent tendency towards chaos which was considered by the ancient Egyptians to be an inherently conflicting principle in the cosmos. The rule of Ma'at had to be enforced and respected by all human beings on earth, from the Pharaoh to each and every Fellah. To respect Ma'at by one's behaviour was understood as a kind of grateful answer of humans towards the beneficial influence of the gods (Erik Hornung).

To respect Ma'at also meant helping to re-establish the permanently threatened cosmic order, and in this way to restore social order and justice again and again.

Today we recognise in this concept of Ma'at the *respect for the divine aspect of Mother Nature and hence for matter.* To our knowledge, the concept of Ma'at is the first setting down of humankind's sustainable relationship with nature and its laws as well as with its relationship to fellow human beings. The concept of Ma'at could be referred to as the *constitution of mankind* (according to Philippe Mastronardi). Any further physical and moral laws would have to orient themselves in accordance with this constitution.

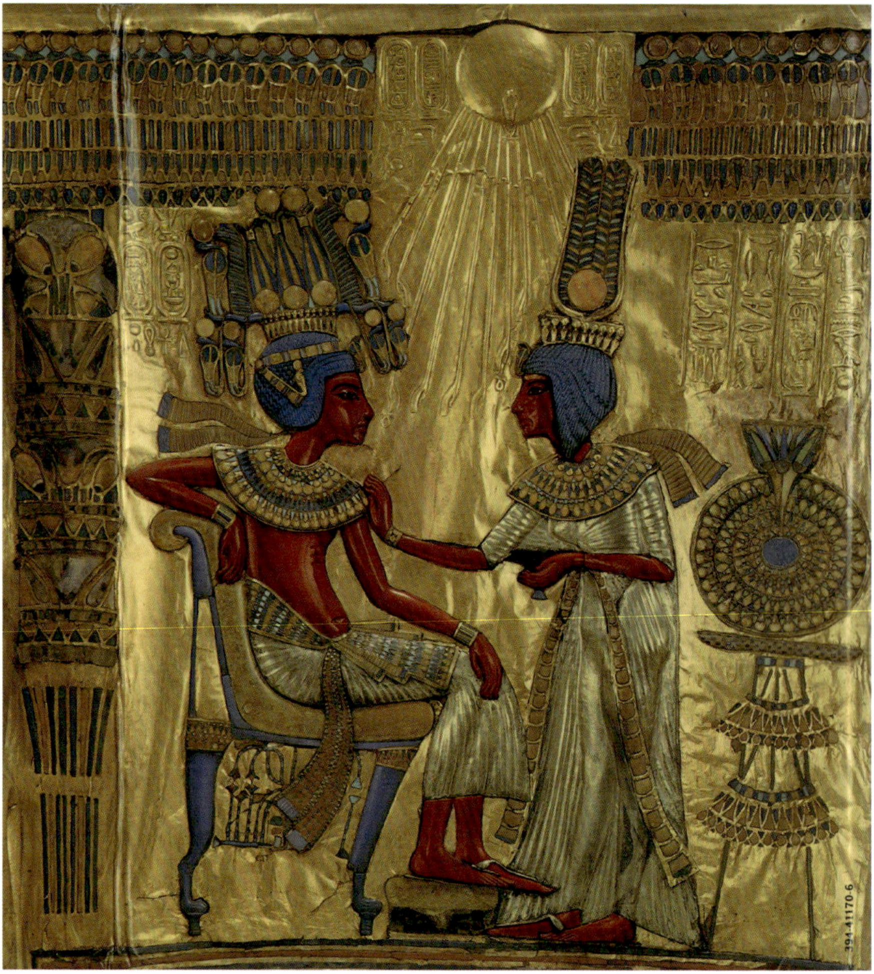

Fig. 7: Decoration of the gilded wooden throne found in the tomb of Tutankhamun. Here we see Tutankhamun and his wife Ankhesenamun being depicted in the Amarna-style. They are protected by the sun-disc representing *Aton*, who was the only god in the Amarna-period, during the rule of Akhenaton (the father of Tutankhamun). *Aton* extends his protecting sunrays to the royal couple. The Egyptian Museum, Cairo JE 62028.

5. Successful Overcoming of a Crisis: Tutankhamun and Ma'at

An amazingly instructive example of the ability of Pharaonic culture to renew and hence rejuvenate itself can be seen in the history of the tomb of Tutankhamun: His father Akhen*aton*, the famous heretic ruler, decided to do away with the many deities, especially the principal divinity, Amun-Re. In a rather fundamental way, he accepted the sun-disc *Aton* as the only god. And he, Akhen*aton* as the supreme ruler, represented Aton on Earth. Akhenaton's Sungod, the light of the sun-disc *Aton*, visible during daytime, overshadowed and ruthlessly removed all the many deities of the night-world.

In the 19th century, the city Akhetaton, which he had built for Aton, was discovered in *Tell el-Amarna*, in Middle Egypt. This is why the reign of Akhenaton is also known today as the Amarna-period.

As in this period the highest and only god was *Aton*, Akhenaton's son was given the birthname Tutankh*aton*. However, when Tutankh*aton* – as a child of around ten years of age – became successor to his father, it was decided to re-establish the traditional belief in the supreme god – Amun-Re – as well as the other many deities of the pre-Amarna-period. His name Tutankh*aton* was therefore changed to Tutankh*amun*. However, in contrast to the one-sided attitude of his father's culture, the innovations and values of the Amarna-period were not simply brushed aside. This meant that the reign of Tutankhamun was able to avoid a break in the continuity of the well-established and proven Pharaonic culture, which is *based on two principles*, namely that of daylight and that of the many night lights. This is an example of the uniting of opposites: the traditional values prevailing before Akhenaton were reconciled with the values of the progressive, innovative father Akhenaton, who, among other things, had accepted for the first time the less perfect features of individual existence, had adopted the language of the people as the official language and had acknowledged the values of foreigners. *Thus Ma'at, the goddess of cosmic order, balance and justice was respected, and the society of Egypt was able to rejuvenate and respect the continuity of its rich culture.*

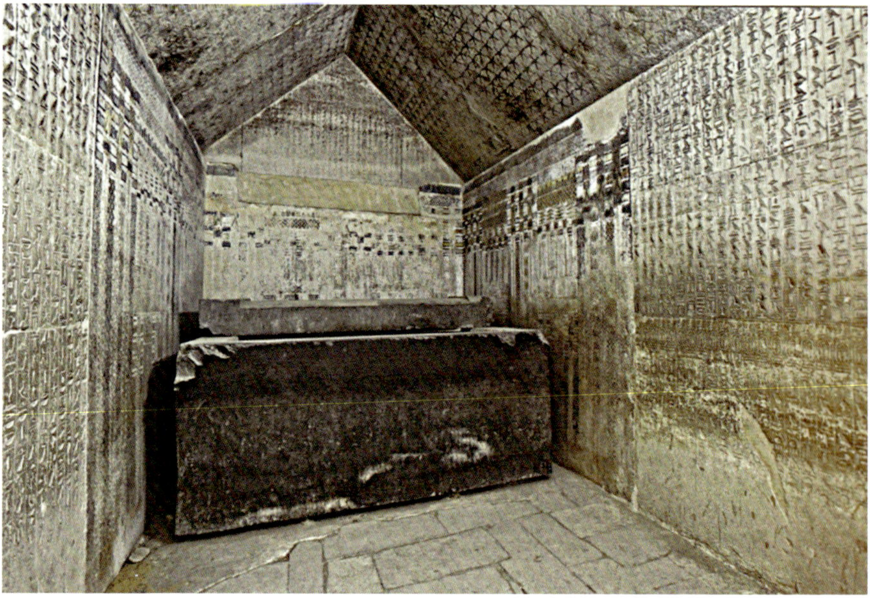

Fig. 8: The oldest religious text known to mankind: The Pyramid texts found in the tomb of Pharaoh Unas (2375-2345 BCE). The text recounts how the Pharaoh becomes immortal after his death through his journey to the northern sky with its never-disappearing stars.

6. The Sungod's Journey to its own eternal Renewal

Pharaonic culture was strongly imbued with a concern for the afterlife, as so many of its monuments, statues and images testify. Very few archaeological traces remain from the daily life of Ancient Egypt. The Egyptians at that time did not focus their main interest in life on earth. They placed the main emphasis on preparation for the world beyond. This is evident in their language: they called their house on earth *rest house* while their tomb was the *house for eternity*.

The ancient Egyptians, with their introverted pondering over the most basic questions of life, created for the first time an *extensive description of the Beyond, which is similar for all human beings*. Today, in the light of modern depth psychology, we recognise in these texts and images the mapping of what today we refer to as the *collective unconscious*.

Pharaonic culture recognised that this "other world", into which humans will enter after death, *has to be known and respected already during lifetime*. In this way, this culture developed a very differentiated view of how the individual can prepare his or her quest for immortality.

As is the case with most cultures on earth, there was more to human life for the ancient Egyptians than mere biological existence. In the early days of Egyptian civilisation, the so-called *Old Kingdom*, the Pharaoh represented the divine on earth. The so-called Pyramid texts, the oldest religious texts known to mankind, recount how the Pharaoh became immortal after his death. At that time the most important thing was that the Pharaoh, on his journey to the sky, would become eternal in the Beyond, like one of those stars that never sink below the horizon. In this way, he was a guarantee for his people that through him they would remain connected with the other world. Later, in the *Middle Kingdom*, such religious texts as these about a journey after death were painted onto the sarcophagi. These are the so-called *Coffin-texts*. Finally, in the *New Kingdom*, at the time of Pharaoh Tutankhamun, this quest for immortality was depicted in the *Amduat* ("What is in the Netherworld"), the earliest complete Egyptian 'guidebook' for the afterlife. This book was intended as a guide for the deceased Pharaoh but, as it is said in the *Amduat*, «this knowledge is not only good for the dead but also for those on earth».

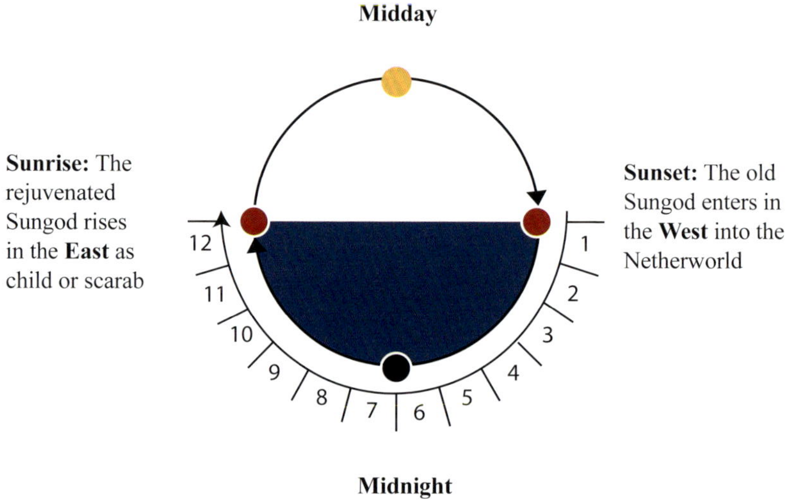

Fig. 9: Diagram of the 12 hours of the night journey of the Sungod. In his barque, he travels on the river Nile, which also flows into the Beyond from the West (sunset) back to the East (sunrise), there to rise rejuvenated.

However, we must bear in mind that although the time axis is divided into 12 hours, for ancient Egyptians, each hour at the same time also represents *the whole Netherworld.*

7. Following the Sungod's Journey can bring about eternal Rejuvenation

From the movement of the sun and of the stars – that each night slowly disappear in the West – human beings can see how these celestial bodies fade away in the West. Thus for the ancient Egyptians, the West became the land of the dead. Like the stars, the sun also disappears in the West in the evening. But in the morning it *rises again* over the eastern horizon, as if completely rejuvenated (Fig. 9). For the ancient Egyptians, the Sungod thus became a role-model for eternal rejuvenation. They saw this never-ending renewal as a possibility *for the human soul as well.*

This is the main idea expressed in text and pictures in the mentioned *Amduat*, a guidebook for the afterlife. It was meant to teach humans about the sun, named in Ancient Egypt the Sungod Re. In the tomb of Tutankhamun, we can find different representations from the *Amduat*, in the burial chamber and on one of the gilded shrines. After the *Amduat*, other Royal Books for the Afterlife followed. They further differentiated this process of the rejuvenation of the Sungod. This quest for immortality was at first only meant to be a task for the Pharaoh. In time, however, this quest came to be shared by nobles and finally, in the late period of Pharaonic culture, this aim became a common goal for humans.

A growth in conscious cognition in Western civilisation about the eternal aspect of human existence has one of its main roots in this Pharaonic culture. At this time, human beings developed an awareness of the potential of a spiritual dimension to their lives, witnessing the relationship to something inside them that would never perish. For our visit to the facsimile of the burial chamber of Tutankhamun, let us keep the following in mind: The mystery of the immortality of the Pharaoh, the son of the Sungod Re, is that in his tomb the deceased Osiris-Tutankhamun can *enter the circular path of his father, the Sungod Re, which will lead him from death to a new birth "in the morning", and thus to the ever rejuvenating circular movement of the Sungod that repeats itself day after day, forever.*

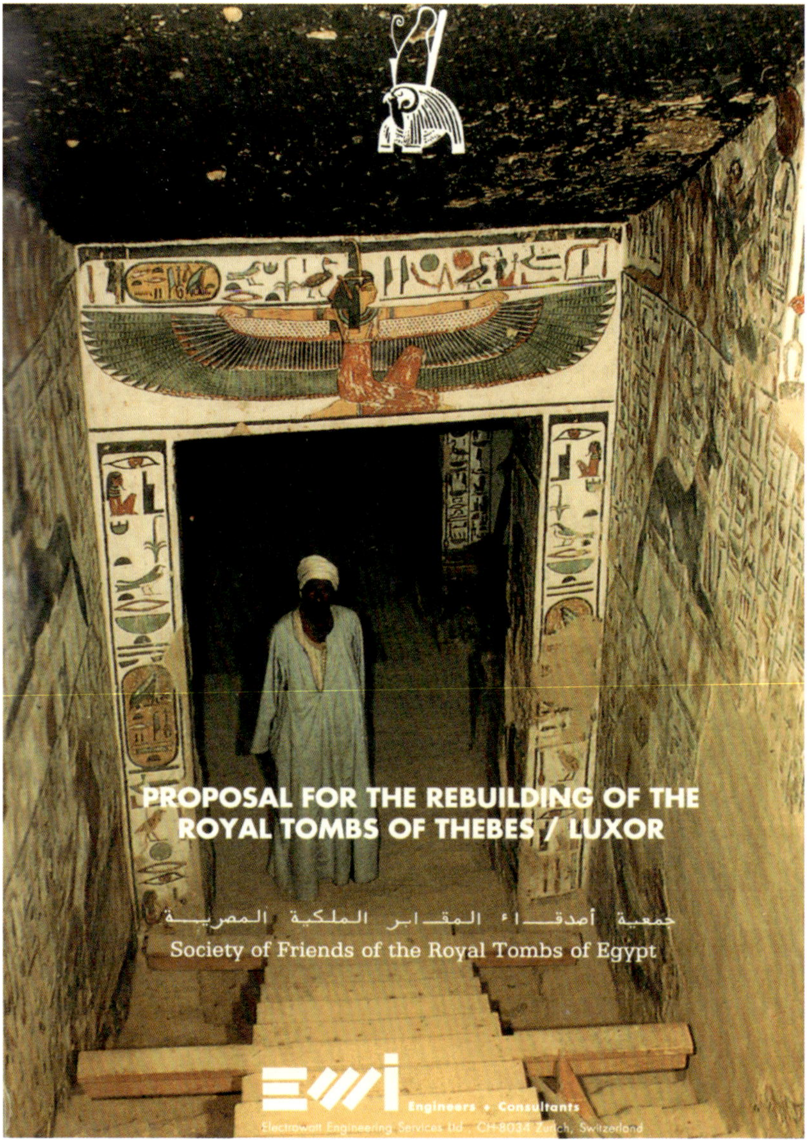

Fig. 10: Proposal for the Rebuilding of the Royal Tombs of Thebes/Luxor by the *Society of Friends of the Royal Tombs of Egypt* (1990).

Part II

The Story of the Creation of Facsimiles of Pharaonic Tombs

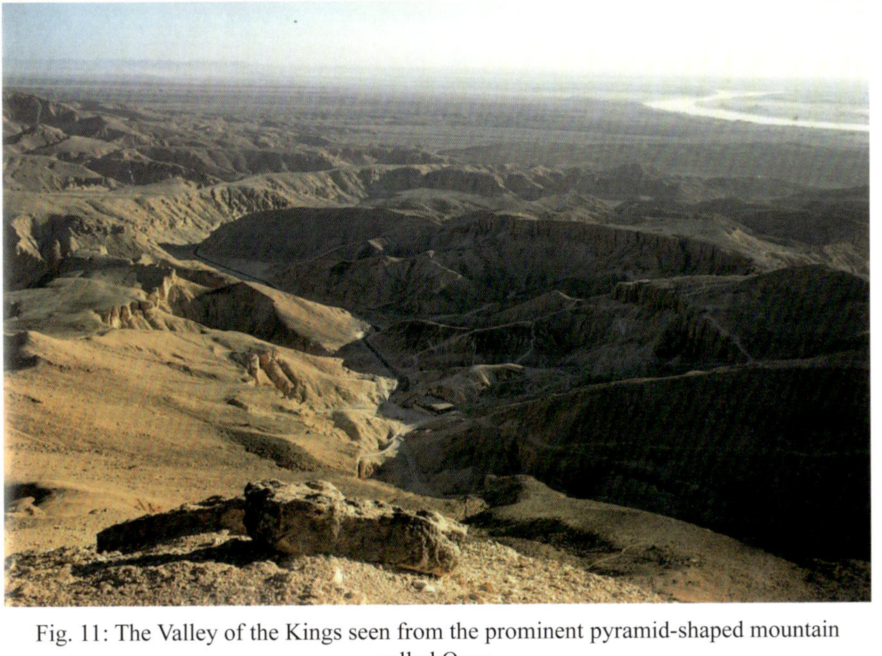

Fig. 11: The Valley of the Kings seen from the prominent pyramid-shaped mountain called Qurn.

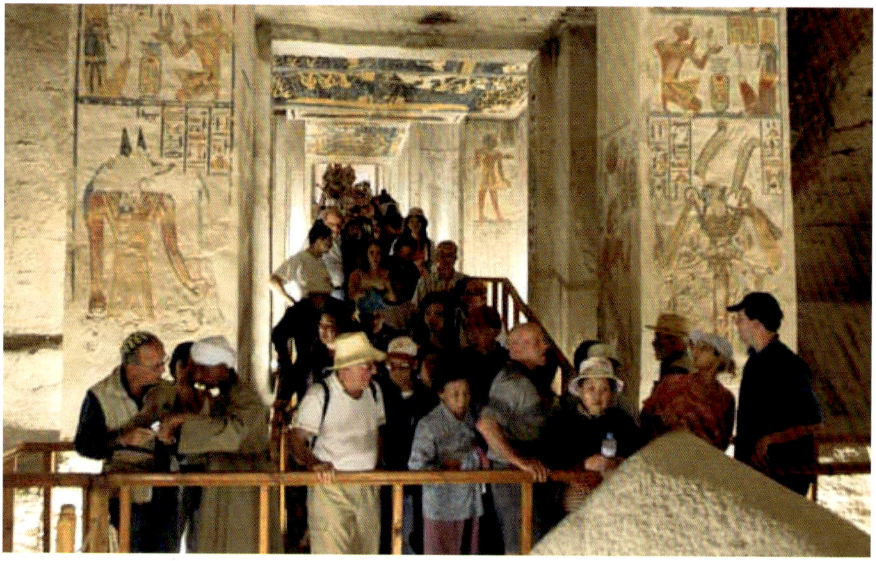

Fig. 12: Visitors to the tomb of Ramses VI.

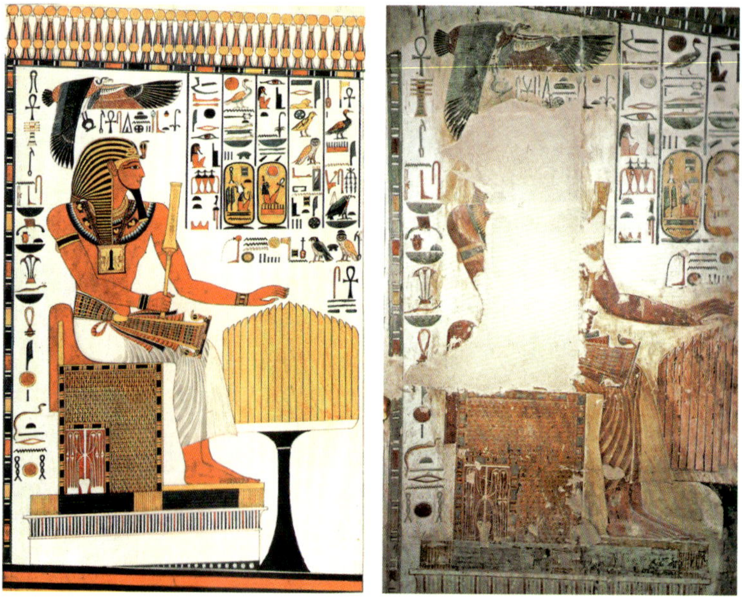

Fig. 13: Pharaoh Seti I in front of an offering table (from the tomb of Seti I). Left image: Painting by Henry Salt in 1818. Right image: Photograph 1999.

1. The Problem of Mass Tourism

Of all the Pharaonic monuments, the Royal tombs in the Valley of the Kings near Luxor in Upper Egypt are among Egypt's oldest and most precious cultural legacies to humanity. These tombs, some of them up to 100 metres in length, were chiselled deep into the rock of this remote desert valley. This was done, as we know, only with the aid of hardened copper and stone tools. Many of the wonderfully decorated walls, corridors and burial chambers still retain their magnificent colour and beauty. Furthermore they have some magical appeal for the visitors that seems to come from a faraway world, unknown to us today, but still somehow near to us. Because of all this, these tombs are especially attractive to visitors from all over the world.

It was a stroke of good fortune for mankind that the site of the tomb of Tutankhamun was discovered by Howard Carter in 1922. The tomb was practically undisturbed for nearly thirty-five hundred years. On the basis of our knowledge of its world-famous treasure, we can only imagine what amazing treasures once must have lain hidden inside these Royal tombs of more imposing Pharaohs buried in the Valley of the Kings. They may have been filled with the most exquisite and beautifully crafted funerary architecture, sculptures and gold, while their walls and corridors have been decorated, as we still can see today.

Today, however, whenever the number of visitors to Egypt again increases, there is a threat to the original tombs, which are visited by people in their hundreds. Temperature changes cause the delicate plaster to expand and contract, and the large number of tourists increases the humidity inside the tombs. The dust visitors produce sticks to the walls and direct contact with the walls can cause serious damage. All of this creates an immediate threat to this wonderful unique human heritage.

Our modern utilitarian mind-set has difficulty in grasping that this huge, labour-intensive endeavour, which began with carving a tomb out of the rock, decorating it with funerary texts and images, and finally filling it with utensils for the afterlife, was *never intended to be seen again by the living.* Building and decorating the tombs was truly a sacred work for the world beyond, a world hidden to all but those who have passed away. This, among others things, can be seen from the title of a workman of the team that created these Royal tombs. He was called *Servant in the Place of Truth (Ma'at).*

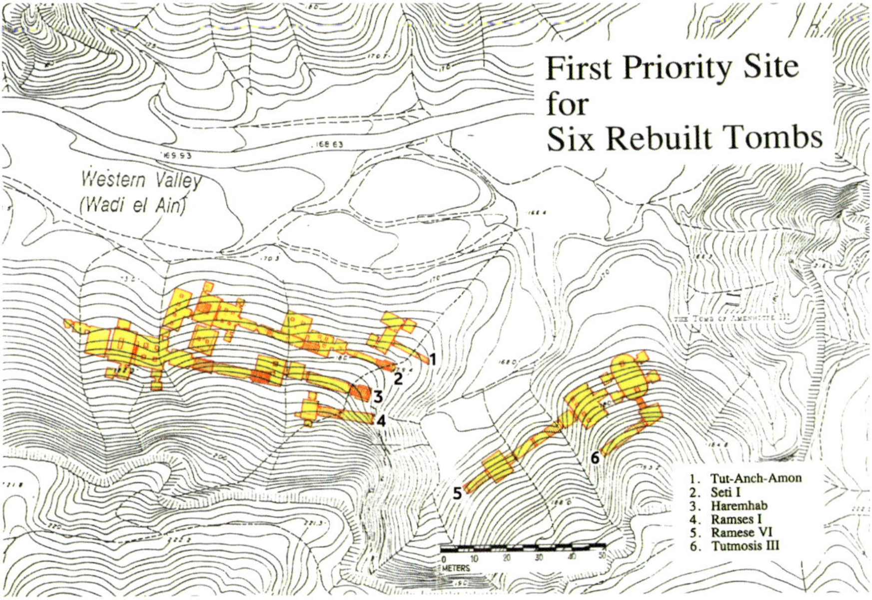

Fig. 14: The six tombs in the King's Valley taken from the proposal of the *Society of Friends of Royal Tombs of Egypt* (1990). The original plan to build the replicas in the western valley had to be changed, because in this area hitherto undiscovered Royal tombs might have been damaged when digging into the mountain.

2. From the Problem to a possible Solution

Realising that tourism could destroy one of Egypt's main attractions and sources of income, and with its protection in mind, the *Society of Friends of the Royal Tombs of Egypt* (SFRT) was established in 1987 with the support of the *Swiss Embassy in Cairo*. In close cooperation with the *Supreme Council of Antiquities* (SCA), known today as the State Ministry of Antiquities, a proposal for the rebuilding of the Royal Tombs of Thebes/Luxor was formulated in 1990 and submitted to the SCA. In the following year, the SFRT was given permission to rebuild the tombs of Pharaoh Tutankhamun and Queen Nefertari.

The main inspiration for this project came from the protection of the prehistoric caves of Lascaux in France, where a facsimile of part of a cave had been rebuilt for visitors. That project became world-famous and was such a success that after the opening of the rebuilt cave, the number of visitors increased four-fold, compared to the number of visitors before the creation of this facsimile.

Inspiration for this project also came from the photographic rebuilding of the tomb of the noble *Sennefer*, a replica that was part of an exhibition in various places in the late 1980s. There was also the painted rebuilding of the tomb of the noble *Sennejem*. Yet neither method of rebuilding a tomb was really able to fulfil the Society's expectations.

In 1991, the President of the *Chamber of Tourism* in Egypt, Elhamy Elzayat, together with key persons in the field of Egyptology – such as Fayza Haykal and Zahi Hawass – as well as people from other fields, such as Tourism, created a *Sister Society of* SFRT in Egypt. An endorsement by UNESCO encouraged SFRT to pursue its efforts to create facsimiles.

In 1985, Paolo and Laura Mora, and their team from the *Getty Conservation Institute* in Los Angeles, obtained permission from the *Egyptian Antiquity Organisation* to restore the endangered paintings of the tomb of *Queen Nefertari*. In 1992, the restoration of this tomb was completed. Thus the tomb could be opened to visitors again. But after a short period it had to be closed to the general public again, as the effect of visitors on conditions in the tomb was considered to be too much of a threat to a long-lasting preservation of the tomb. *Restoration is obviously no solution to the sustainable protection of this unique human heritage.*

In 1996, a symposium in the Cairo Opera was organised by the SFRT and the Swiss Embassy in order to open up the discussion about how to ensure lasting protection of the Royal tombs. Following this symposium, the idea of rebuilding the Royal tombs was unfortunately *rejected by sceptics, their argument being that nobody would be interested in visiting replicas.*

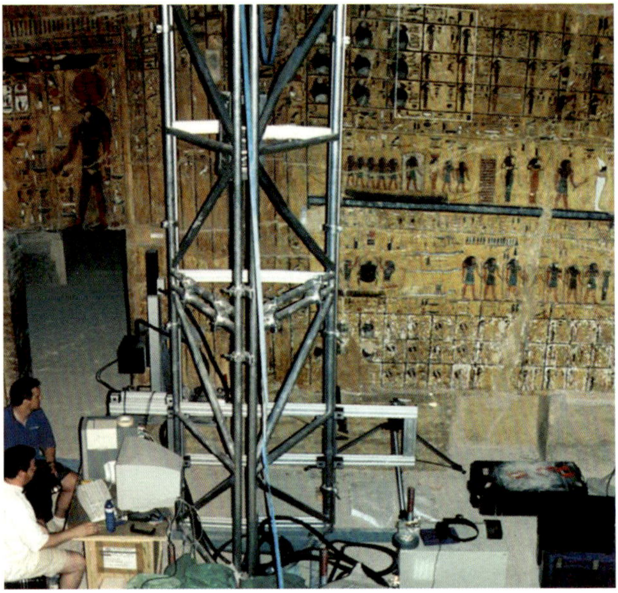

Fig. 15: People from *Factum Arte* in the tomb of Pharaoh Seti I.

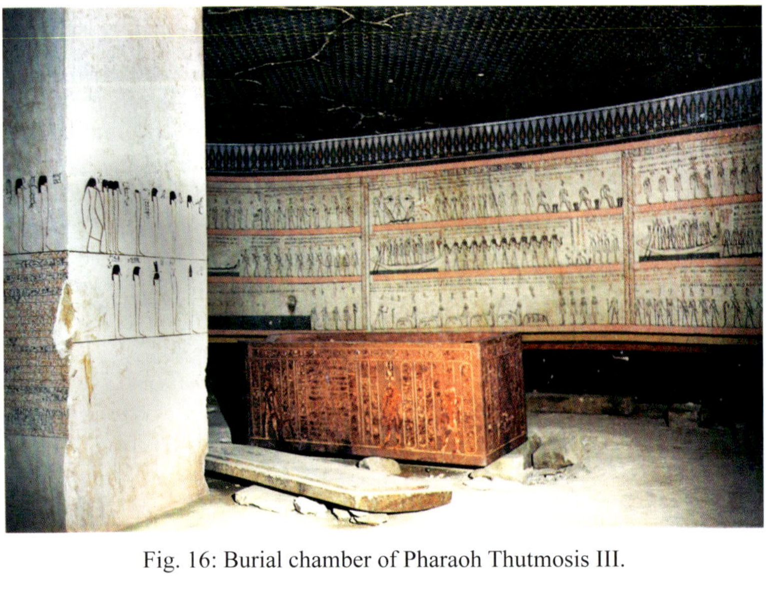

Fig. 16: Burial chamber of Pharaoh Thutmosis III.

3. The Facsimile of the Tomb of Thutmosis III

In order to convince these sceptics that the rebuilding of the Royal tombs could attract visitors, the *Society of Friends of the Royal Tombs of Egypt* initiated the creation of an exhibition in the year 2000, organised by *United Exhibits* in Copenhagen. The exhibition was entitled "Quest for Immortality – Treasures of Ancient Egypt". The idea was that it would tour major cities in the United States and in Europe.

By some undoubtedly meaningful coincidence, when the *United Exhibits* team was in Luxor, it was able to meet the team of *Factum Arte* from Madrid.

Independent of the society's project, *Factum Arte* had already started a project to scan the tomb of Pharaoh Seti I (see fig. 15), approved by the *Supreme Council of Antiquities* (SCA). This allowed *Factum Arte* to develop technology enabling them accurately to scan the high-relief paintings of this tomb in three dimensions.

The outcome of the above-mentioned meeting was an agreement that for the exhibition "Quest for Immortality", *Factum Arte* would create the first 1:1 facsimile of a Pharaonic tomb. The tomb of Thutmosis III was the one chosen. Unfortunately the scanning of the tomb of Seti I had to be abandoned shortly after this meeting, owing to financial problems.

In 2002, Factum Arte was able to complete the exact facsimile of the tomb of Pharaoh Thutmosis III for the touring exhibition "Quest for Immortality". This facsimile demonstrated the high level of accuracy that can be achieved when the application of sophisticated technology is combined with high levels of manual and mechanical skill.

The facsimile of the tomb of Thutmosis III became the star attraction of the exhibition, thus also highlighting the need for the lasting preservation of and accessibility to these wonders, a unique witness of the past. Almost 3 million people have visited this facsimile. *This was convincing proof that a facsimile of such a wonderful and mysterious human heritage can also have a magic of its own.*

As we only protect what we recognise as valuable, a book was created with regard to the decoration of the burial chamber of the tomb of Pharaoh Thutmosis III. This book, *Knowledge for the Afterlife* (by Th. Abt and E. Hornung), aims at pointing out the possible *meaning* of the decoration programme of this Royal tomb. It was written in the hope to attract interest to the timeless value of its depiction of the structure of the Beyond, a gift of Ancient Egypt to our time. It is something that humans need to know today.

MESSAGE FROM THE SECRETARY GENERAL OF THE SUPREME COUNCIL OF ANTIQUITIES

I have often said I believe that the tombs of the pharaohs in the Valley of the Kings could be completely destroyed from modern activities in less than one hundred years. But there are tombs that we can replicate, which contain magical, beautiful scenes. These tombs are the tomb of Tutankhamun, the tomb of Seti I and the tomb of the great queen Nefertari.

Therefore, I am supporting this important project to create facsimiles of these great tombs in order to save the originals. People can visit the exact replicas and experience the beauty of these tombs and know that they are preserving the past.

I wish this fund-raising campaign the best of success.

Zahi Hawass

Dr Zahi Hawass
Secretary General of the
Supreme Council of Antiquities

Society of Friends of the Royal Tombs of Egypt
Munsterhof 16, 8001 Zurich, Switzerland
Tel +41 44 211 0535
Mob +41 76 419 0535
theodor.abt@env.ethz.ch

Fig. 17: The message of the Secretary General of the *Supreme Council of Antiquities*.

4. The Facsimile of the Tomb of Tutankhamun

In 2008, the *University of Basel* and the *Society of Friends of the Royal Tombs* were given approval by the Permanent Committee of the *Supreme Council of Antiquities* of Egypt, headed by Dr. Zahi Hawass, to create, together with *Factum Arte* in Madrid, a facsimile of the tomb of Seti I.

However, because there was too much dust in the tomb of Seti I – as a result of archaeological research going on in this tomb – it was decided to start the three-dimensional recording in the tomb of Tutankhamun.

This turned out to be a piece of good luck, as this tomb is not only much smaller but also world-famous, because it is virtually the only Royal tomb in Egypt that has not been plundered. As it is a small tomb, the creation of a facsimile of this tomb was accomplished in a relatively short period of time.

In March 2009, *Factum Arte* from Madrid was able to start work. With the help of specially developed scanners for digital mapping, its team was able to document the whole tomb. Thus the tomb was recorded with previously unimaginable levels of accuracy in colour and three-dimensional.

Afterwards, in the years 2011/12, again with specially developed technology, *Factum Arte* was able to build the facsimile of the tomb of Tutankhamun with a degree of accuracy that was, in its day, both unique and ground-breaking.

In this facsimile, it was also possible to recreate the wall which had to be destroyed by the archaeologist Howard Carter, in order to remove the golden shrines inside the burial chamber. Thus the scanning technique of *Factum Arte* allowed the tomb to be completely reconstructed almost as it had been when it was discovered. When it was rebuilt in 2014, close to the excavation house of Howard Carter, it *was presented to the people of Egypt as a gift*.

The immensely sophisticated and costly work was possible thanks to the technical skill of *Factum Arte* and the generous support of the *Foundation for Digital Technology in Conservation* – created specifically for this project – and to smaller contributions from the *Society of Friends of the Royal Tombs of Egypt*.

Having started off as a private initiative, financed without any public funding, this project shows that the preservation of significant cultural heritage can inspire individuals to contribute to this important task, namely to support *the continuity of culture*.

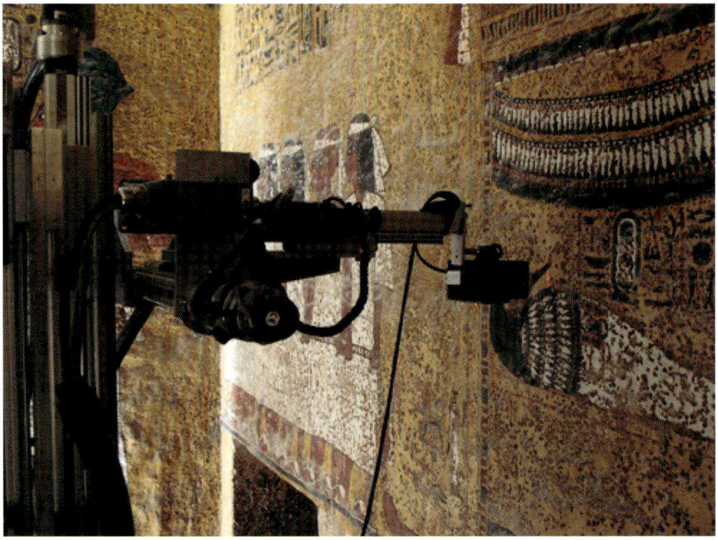

Fig. 18: Scanning of the east wall of the tomb of Tutankhamun.

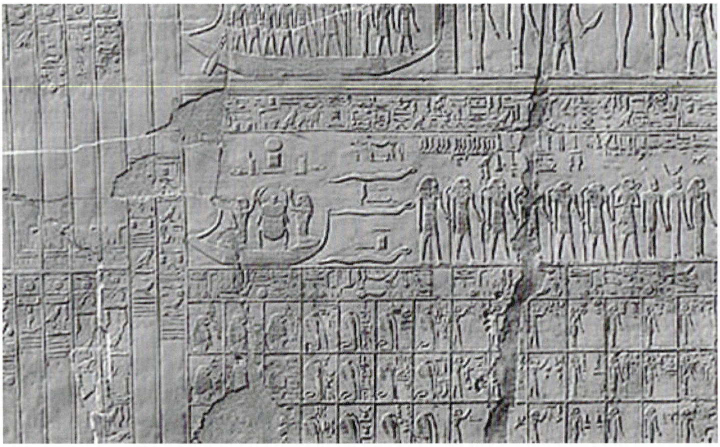

Fig. 19: The tiles, printed in three dimensions, were taken to the warehouses of *Factum Arte* in Madrid where they were rendered together. The aim was to imperceptibly merge all the routed tiles, which called for skilled craftsmanship as well as traditional techniques, in order to complement the digital process. Here we see the surface of a wall of the tomb of Seti I, with a pronounced relief, showing a part of the first hour of the *Amduat*.

5. The Phases of Making the Facsimile of the Tomb of Tutankhamun

a. Step I: Scanning and reproduction of the original tomb

The team of *Factum Arte*, with its director Adam Lowe, did this part of the work, initially in the Valley of the Kings and then in their headquarters in Madrid.

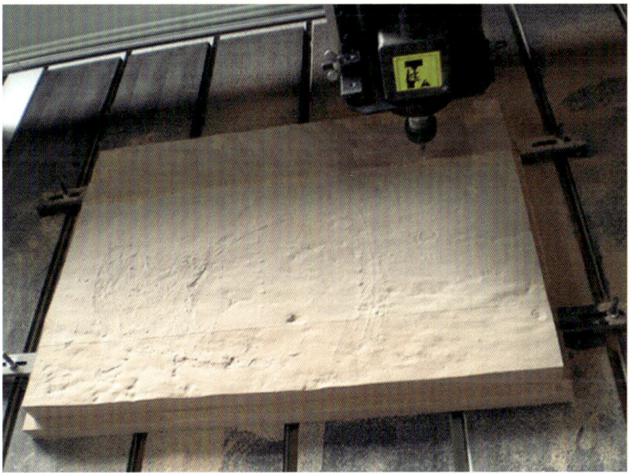

Fig. 20: Routing of the scanned 3D-image on a tile: The high resolution 3D-data are converted and sent to a CNC milling machine, which – piece by piece – cuts out the corresponding routed surface into a block of polyurethane.

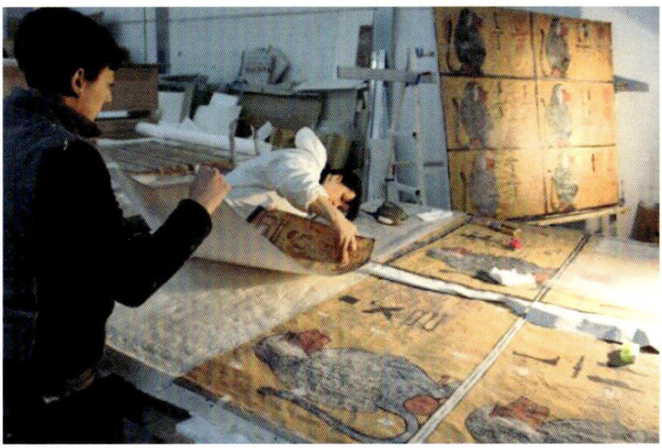

Fig. 21: In the next step, the colour is matched and printed onto a flexible skin-like layer, which is applied to the merged tiles. Here, a part of the west wall with baboons, from the tomb of Tutankhamun.

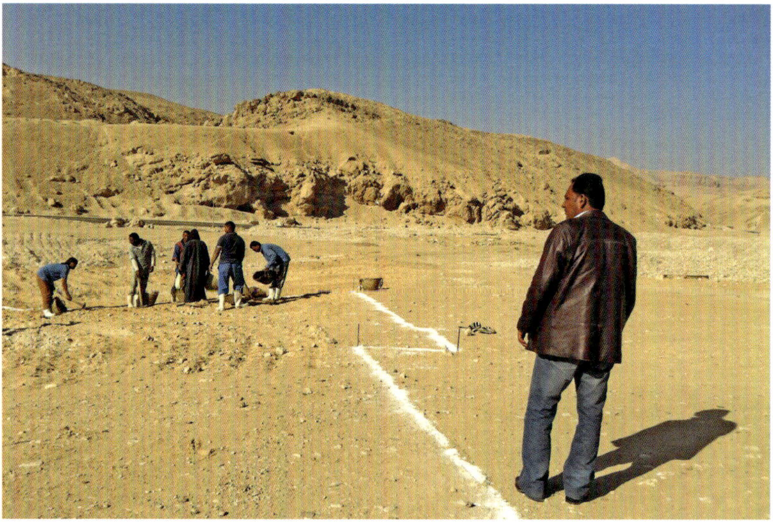

Fig. 22: The new tomb is being excavated in the traditional way: with an outline made of chalk, and then dug out by manual labour. Machines are not allowed on antiquity land.

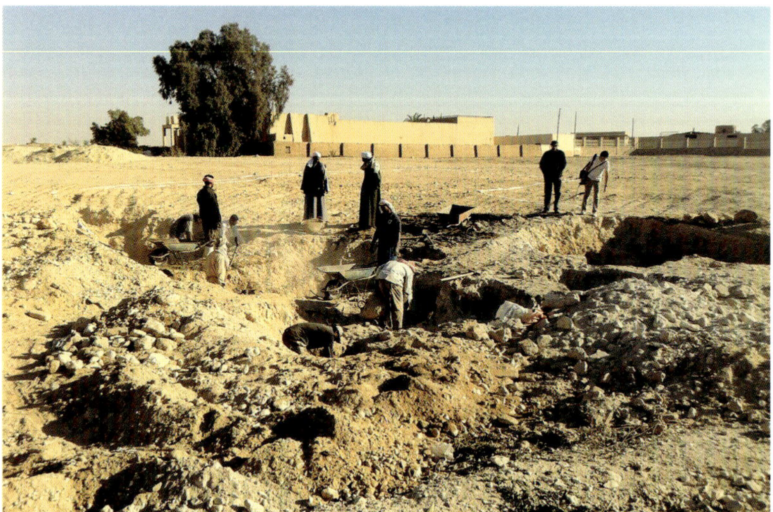

Fig. 23: With axes and spades, an open den is dug into the soil, consisting of debris, stones and sand. The excavated material is carried away with baskets and wheelbarrows.

b. Step II: Digging and building the underground container for the rebuilt tomb

The second part of this work was carried out by the *Tarek Waly Centre* under the direction of Dr Tarek Waly. It was created next to Carter's house, at the entrance to the Valley of the Kings (see fig. 39). Being an Egyptian team, they were well able to deal with the problems occurring during construction on land belonging to the *Ministry of Antiquities*. As one never knows what will appear when one is starting to dig into the soil of antiquity land, no machinery was allowed. Thus all the work had to be executed in the traditional way – as on an excavation site – with shovel and basket.

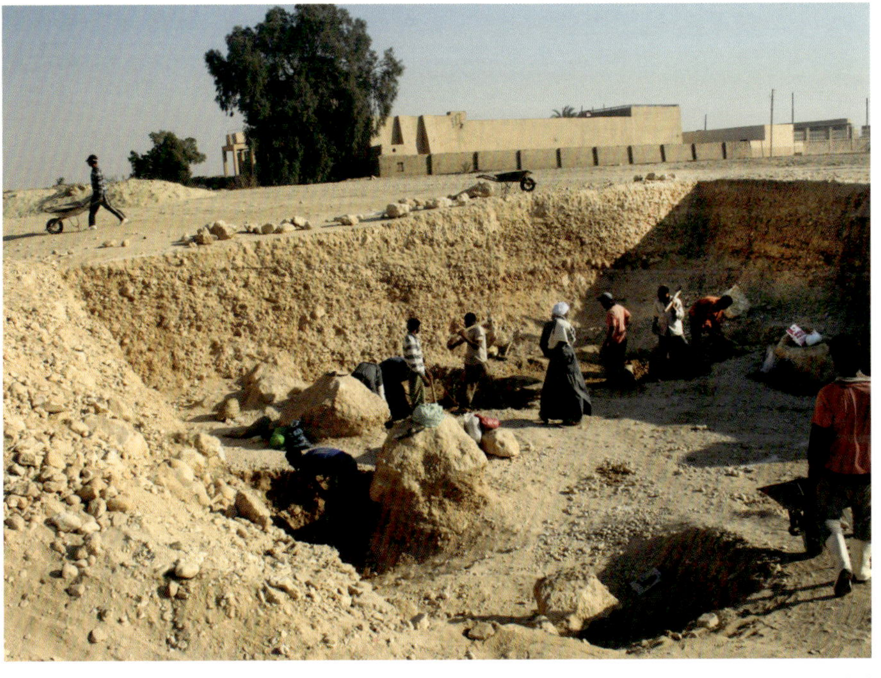

Fig. 24: After some two months of digging, the den is almost finished. It was to be roofed later. The aim was to create an underground building for the exact facsimile of the Tomb of Tutankhamun, at the entrance to the Valley of the Kings.

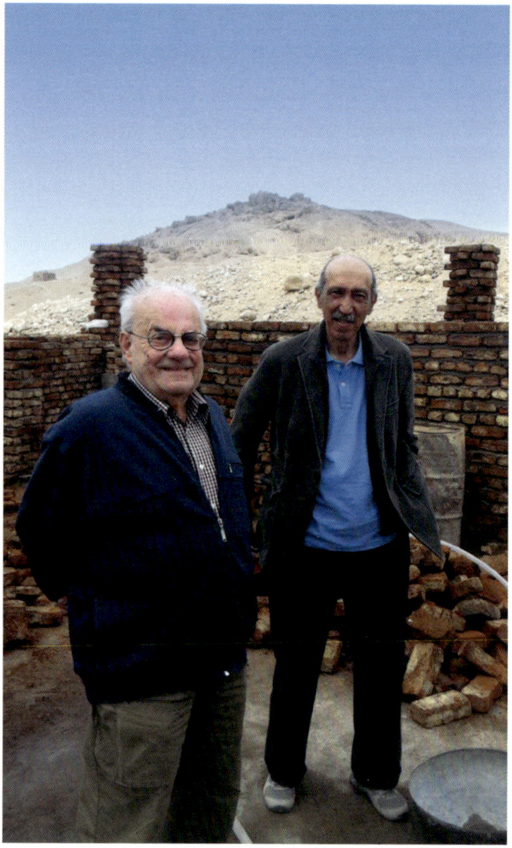

Fig. 25: In the next step, brick walls were constructed to the exact measurements of the walls of the original tomb. On the left, Egyptologist and vice-president of the *Society of Friends of the Royal Tombs of Egypt,* Prof. Dr Erik Hornung; on the right, architect Dr Tarek Waly.

As the *Society of Friends of the Royal Tombs of Egypt* had also worked on a project in Abydos for many years, this led to a common project with Dr Tarek Waly. This project, with the title "Reconciliation with the past, a development project for Abydos", was submitted to the *Supreme Council of Antiquities* in 2006. Meanwhile the *Tarek Waly Centre* was able to create the new visitor centre in Abydos. Owing to the revolution, however, the project could only be completed in 2015.

The collaboration with the team of Tarek Waly established the reputation of the skills and the philosophy of the *Tarek Waly Centre.* Thus, when it came to the building of this container for the facsimile of the tomb of Tutankhamun, the *Tarek Waly Centre* could be warmly recommended for the collaboration with *Factum Arte.*

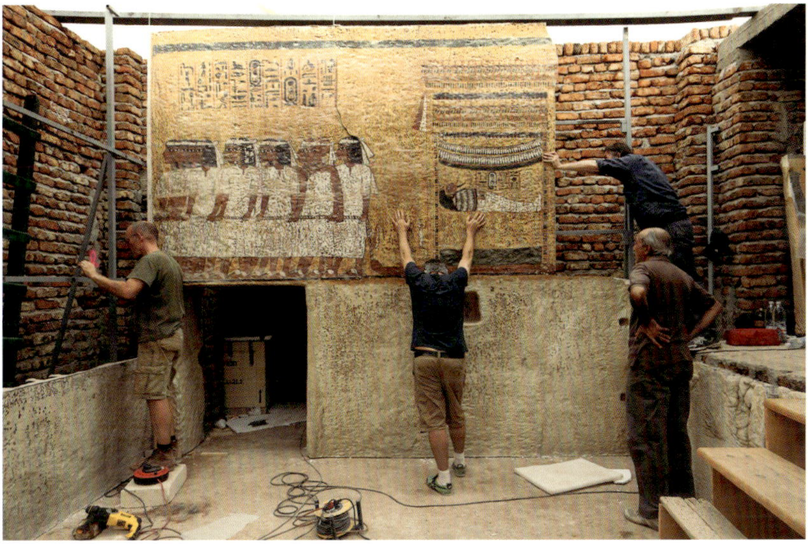

Fig. 26: Onto these walls the panels of the facsimile were erected in the underground chamber. (Left, Mike Roberts; centre, Mike Ward; top right, Adam Lowe; all *Factum Arte*). The architect Dr Tarek Waly of the *Tarek Waly Centre* is the supervisor.

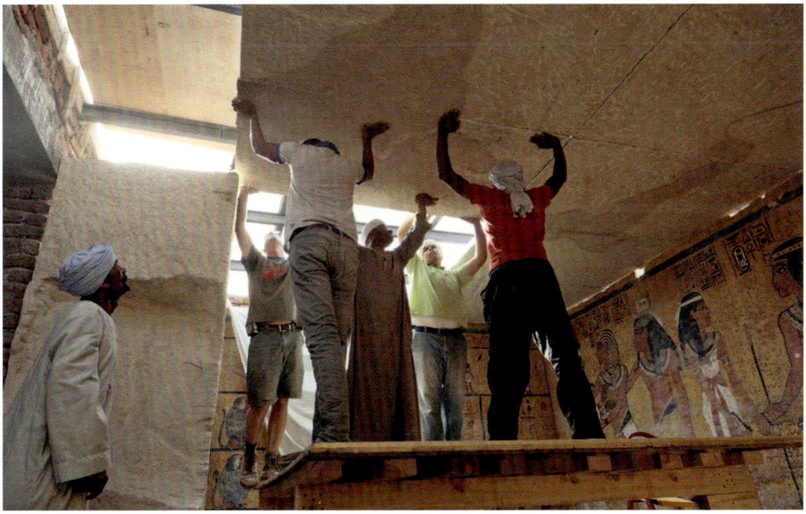

Fig. 27: For the ceiling, members of the installation team from *Factum Arte* had to physically move the panels into place. The complete ceiling weighs nearly 2.5 tons and creates an authentic subterranean sensation.

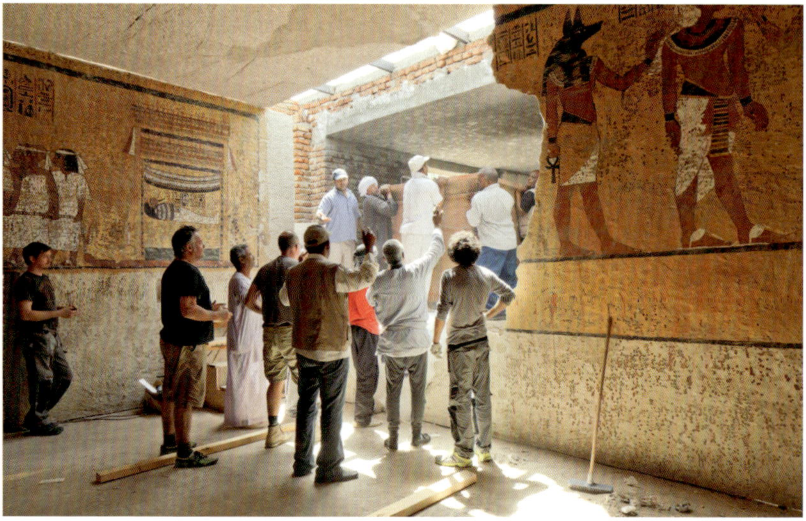

Fig. 28: The rebuilt sarcophagus of Tutankhamun was carried through the opening that Carter had to create by force when he removed the gilded shrines from the tomb.

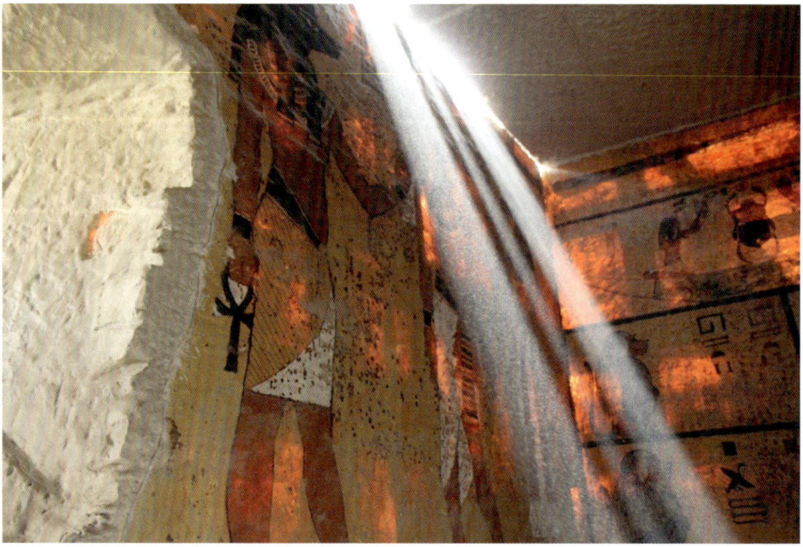

Fig. 29: Through a gap between roof and wall, light still shines into the burial chamber, lighting up the west wall of the rebuilt tomb.

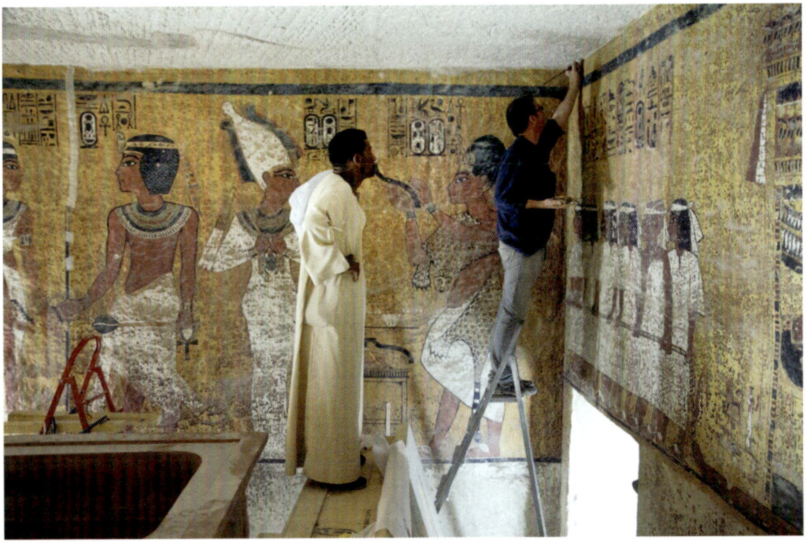

Fig. 30: The gap has been closed and adjustments are made to the walls and their joints.

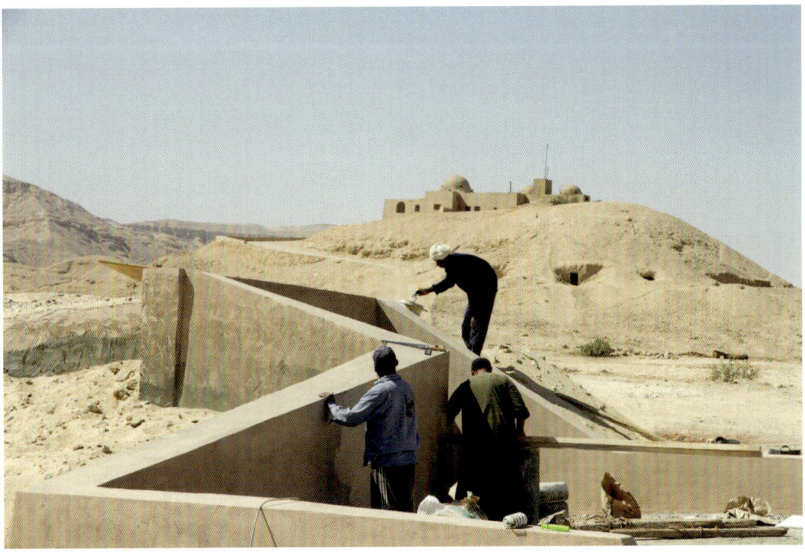

Fig. 31: Completing the entrance to the facsimile of the Tutankhamun tomb. On the hill is the Stoppelaëre house, built by the famous Egyptian architect Hassan Fathy.

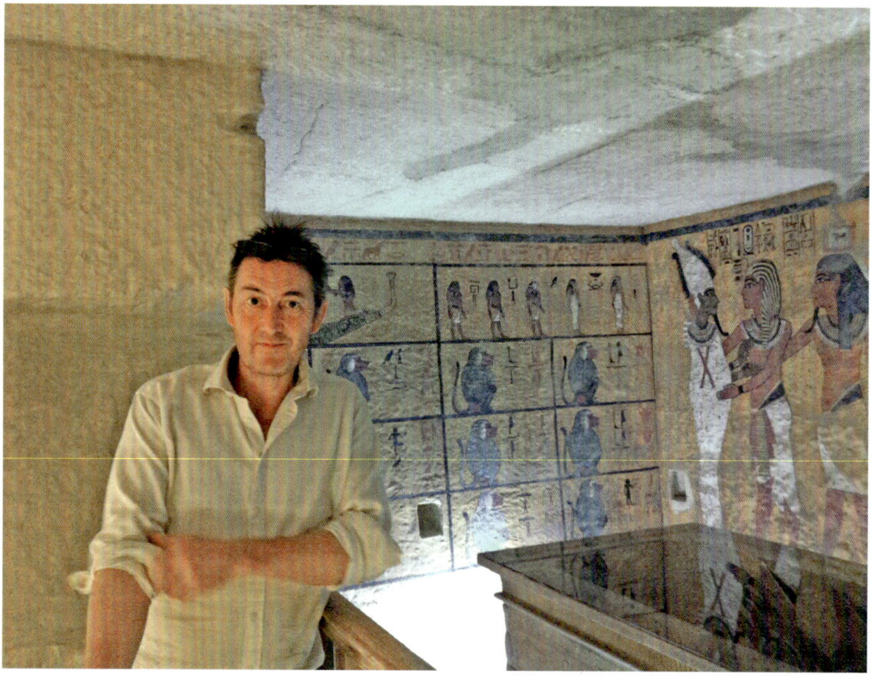

Fig. 32: The interior of the facsimile of the tomb with its sarcophagus, seen from the visitor's perspective. In front: Adam Lowe, director of *Factum Arte.* The interior is lit as in the original before air conditioning was installed, by means of simple fluorescent tubes.

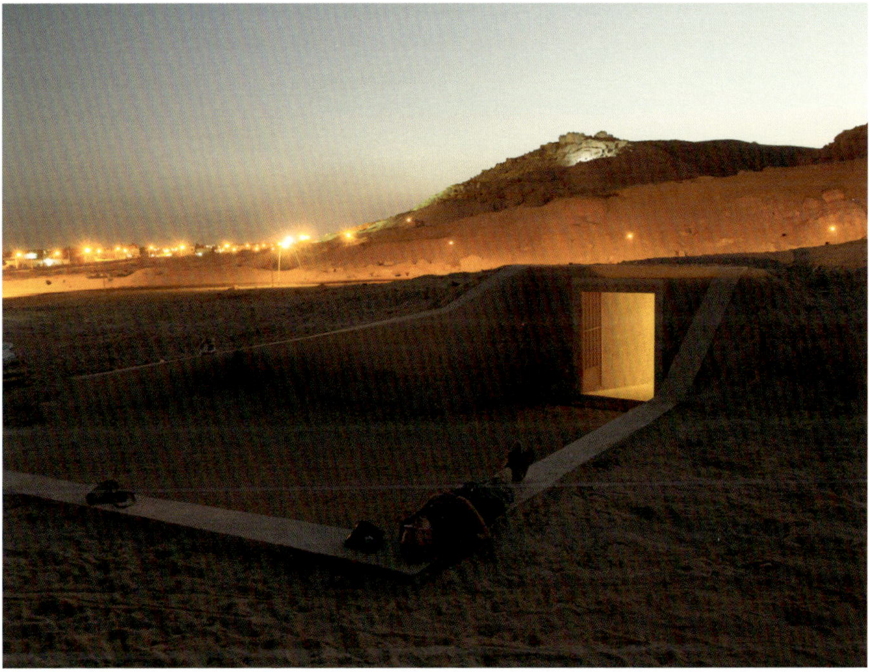

Fig. 33: The exterior of the tomb recreates the impression of going into the earth, visiting a real tomb. Here, in the evening, with the lights of the valley road in the background.

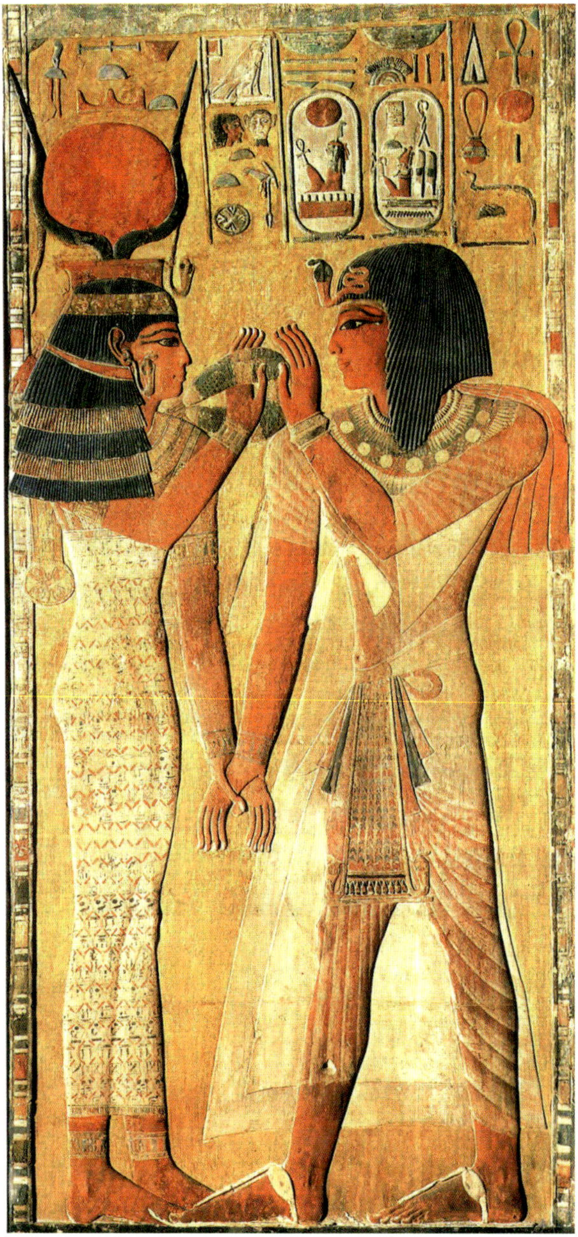

Fig. 34: Pharaoh Seti I in front of the goddess Hathor. From the tomb of Seti I.

This scene was cut out of the tomb in 1828 by Champollion and is now to be seen in the Louvre in Paris. A facsimile, made of this scene and many more removed scenes and fragments, can be inserted into the facsimile of the tomb of Seti I.

6. The Facsimiles of the Tombs of Seti I and Queen Nefertari

The next milestone for the Society of Friends of the Royal Tombs of Egypt is to support Factum Arte, Factum Foundation and the Tarek Waly Centre, under the umbrella of the University of Basel in Switzerland to carry out the recording and creation of a facsimile of the tomb of Pharaoh Seti I. In winter 2015 the contract for the rebuilding of this tomb could be signed by the Minister of Antiquities and the University of Basel.

This tomb of Seti I has been closed to visitors *since more than twenty years* for reasons of security and preservation. It is over 100 metres long, penetrating deep into the rock of the mountain in the Valley of the Kings. It is decorated with outstanding, coloured scenes in high relief. The decoration covers a surface of around 2,300 m^2. This tomb is considered to be the most beautiful in the Valley of the Kings.

For this tomb of Seti I, it will be possible to present the facsimile with the inclusion of dozens of fragments that were cut out of the tomb in the 19th century and then shipped to different museums around the world (see example in fig. 34). Over many years, the whereabouts of a great amount of such fragments have been identified by Prof. Dr Erik Hornung and then also by Dr Florence Barberio. Thus the facsimile will be more complete than the present original and hence closer to its state in when it was discovered by Giovanni Battista Belzoni in 1817.

The facsimile of Seti I with its high-relief coloured decoration will be digitally recorded in three dimensions with an accuracy of one tenth of a millimeter. The cost of this huge facsimile will be significant. The concept is to build it in Luxor, bringing vitally needed skills to the area.

Next, or even at the same time if the financial means permit, the task of creating the facsimile of the tomb of Queen Nefertari has to be undertaken. As already mentioned, this most beautiful tomb was restored between 1985-1992 by the Getty Foundation. Shortly afterwards, however, it had to be closed to the general public in order to protect its unique decoration from deterioration (see fig. 2 on p. 10).

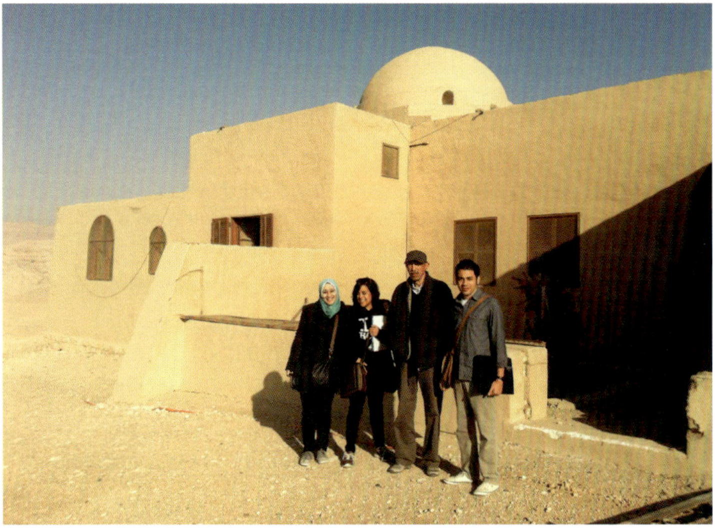

Fig. 35: The abandoned house of Alexandre Stoppelaëre, where a Centre for Education will be set up. In the foreground: The architect Dr Tarek Waly with members of the *Tarek Waly Centre*. (All the photos of Stoppelaëre's house shown here were taken in January 2014.)

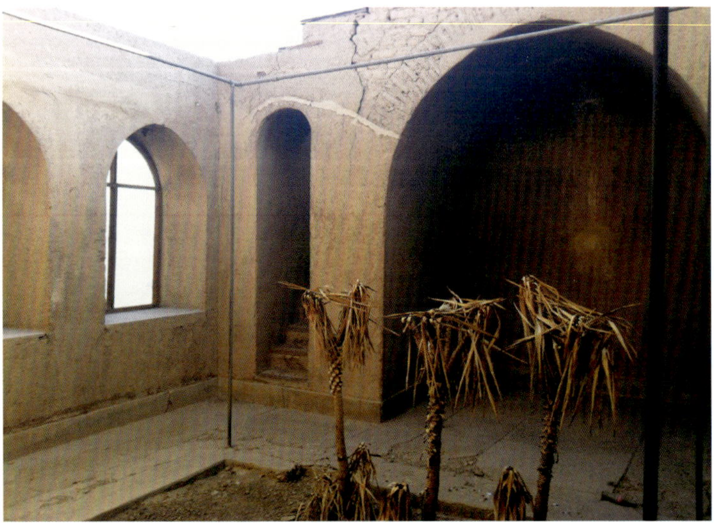

Fig. 36: One of the inner courtyards of Stoppelaëre's house.

7. Creating Work-places for Egyptians

A further important aim of this project is to create jobs for Egyptians. The transfer of technology and know-how from *Factum Arte* to Luxor will be of central importance. To this end, the setting-up of a *Centre for Education* is planned in a house situated on the hill near Carter's house and the facsimile of the tomb of Pharaoh Tutankhamun. It is a house that was built by the famous Egyptian architect Hassan Fathy. It has been abandoned for over twenty years and will need urgent restoration.

The Centre (see pictures on the left) that has been planned together with the facsimile of the tomb of Tutankhamun is expected to become a part of the visitor's programme. In this way, the tourist will learn how facsimiles are created and be made aware of how accurate they are, thanks to modern technology.

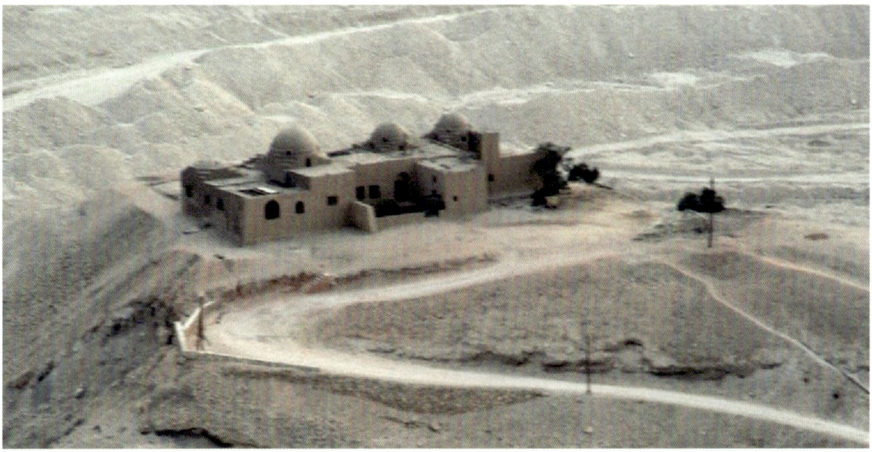

Fig. 37: Bird's eye view of the abandoned Stoppelaëre house, where a Centre for 3-D Scanning and Training will be created. The architect was the famous Hassan Fathy, and the restoration will be done by Tarek Waly who had worked together with Hassan Fathy.

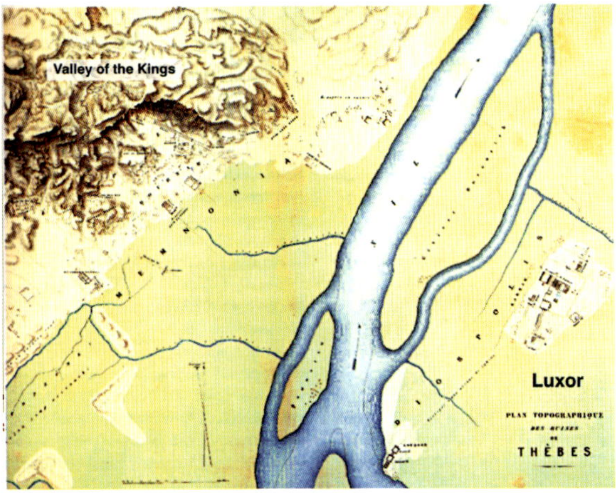

Fig. 38: Ancient map of Luxor and the West bank with the Valley of the Kings in the mountain area.

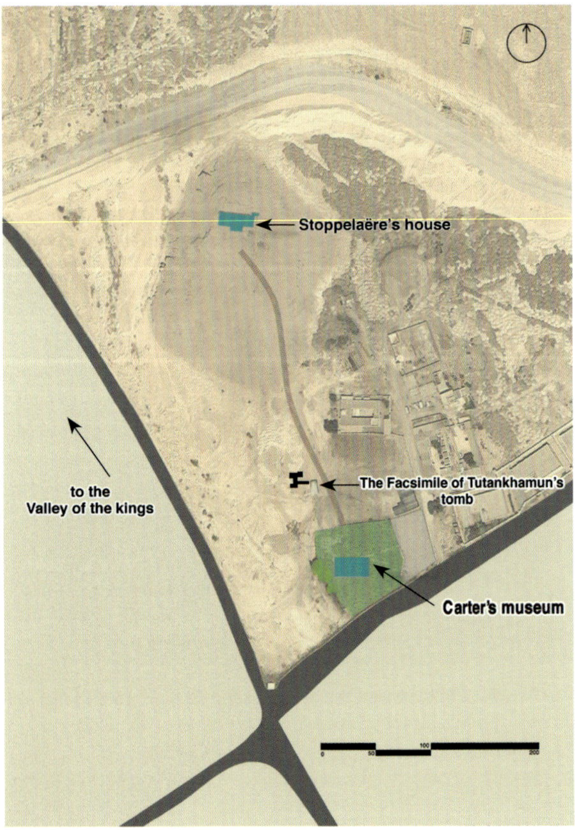

Fig. 39: The location of Stoppelaëre's house, some 300 metres from the facsimile of the tomb of Tutankhamun and the Carter house that is today Carter's Museum.

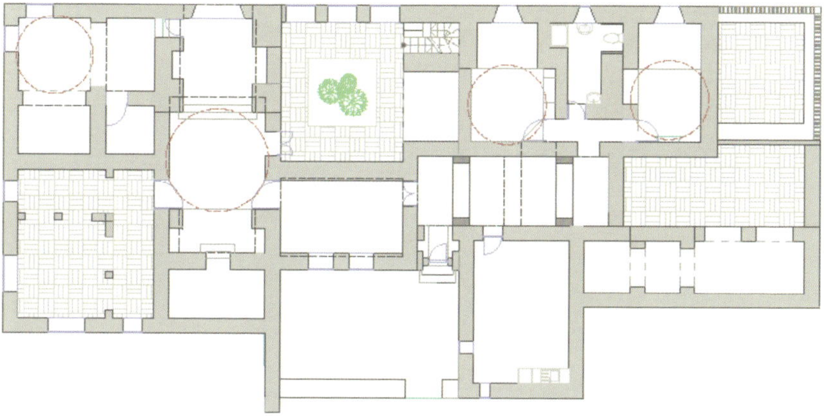

Fig. 40: Architectural plan of the Stoppelaëre house, with some 300m^2 of space to be used for a Centre for Training for 3-D Scanning.

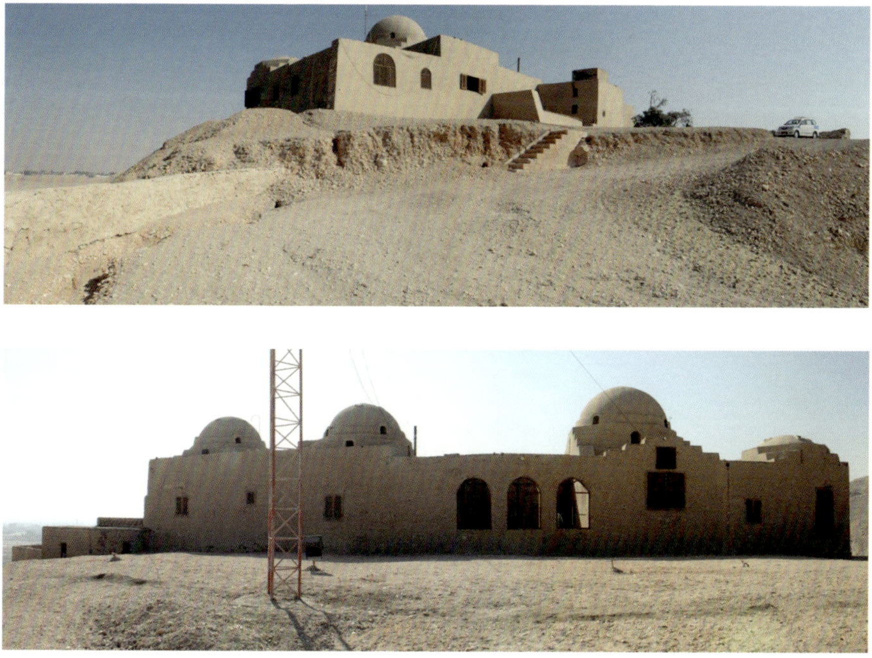

Fig. 41: The Stoppelaëre house seen (above) from the South, and (below) from the North.

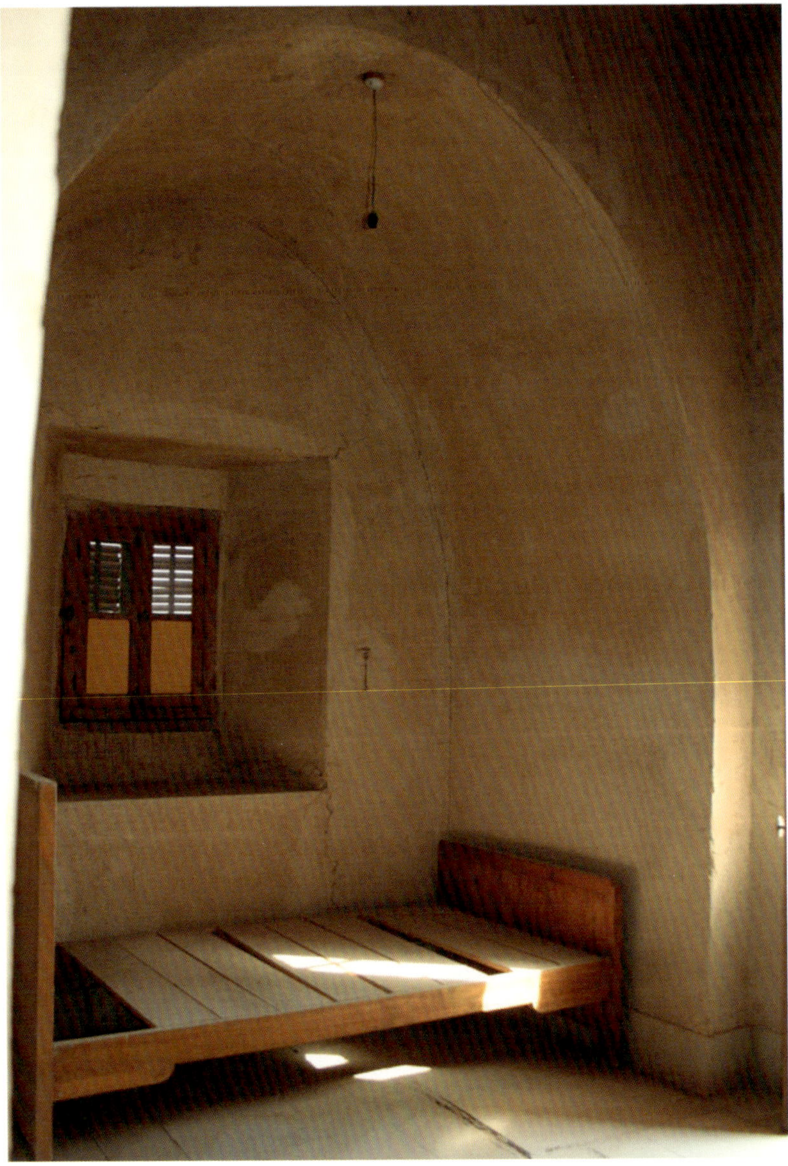

Fig. 42: The interior of the Stoppelaëre house. The house, built of mud bricks, has a unique atmosphere.

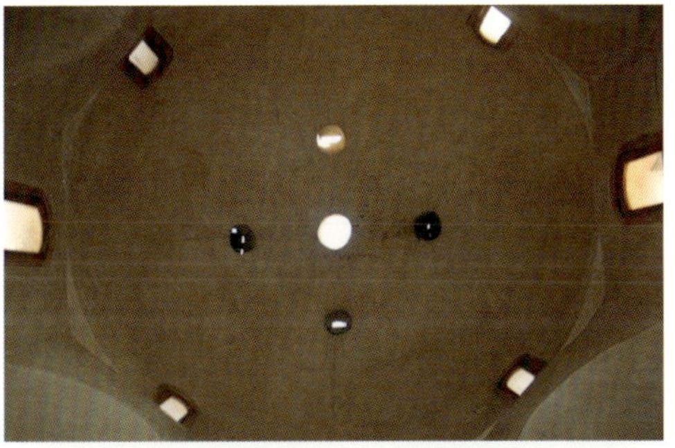

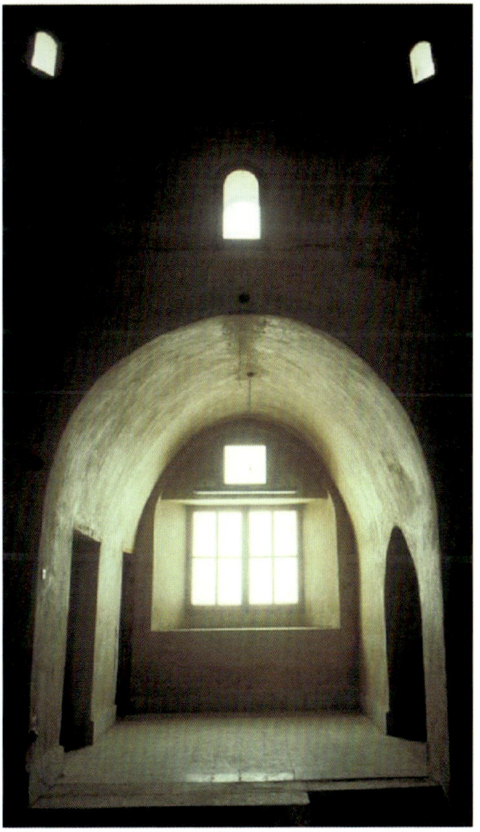

Fig. 43: Inside the Stoppelaëre house. The house has a natural, traditional air-cooling system. The renovation of such a house requires experts skilled in these traditional techniques which can be provided by the *Tarek Waly Centre*.

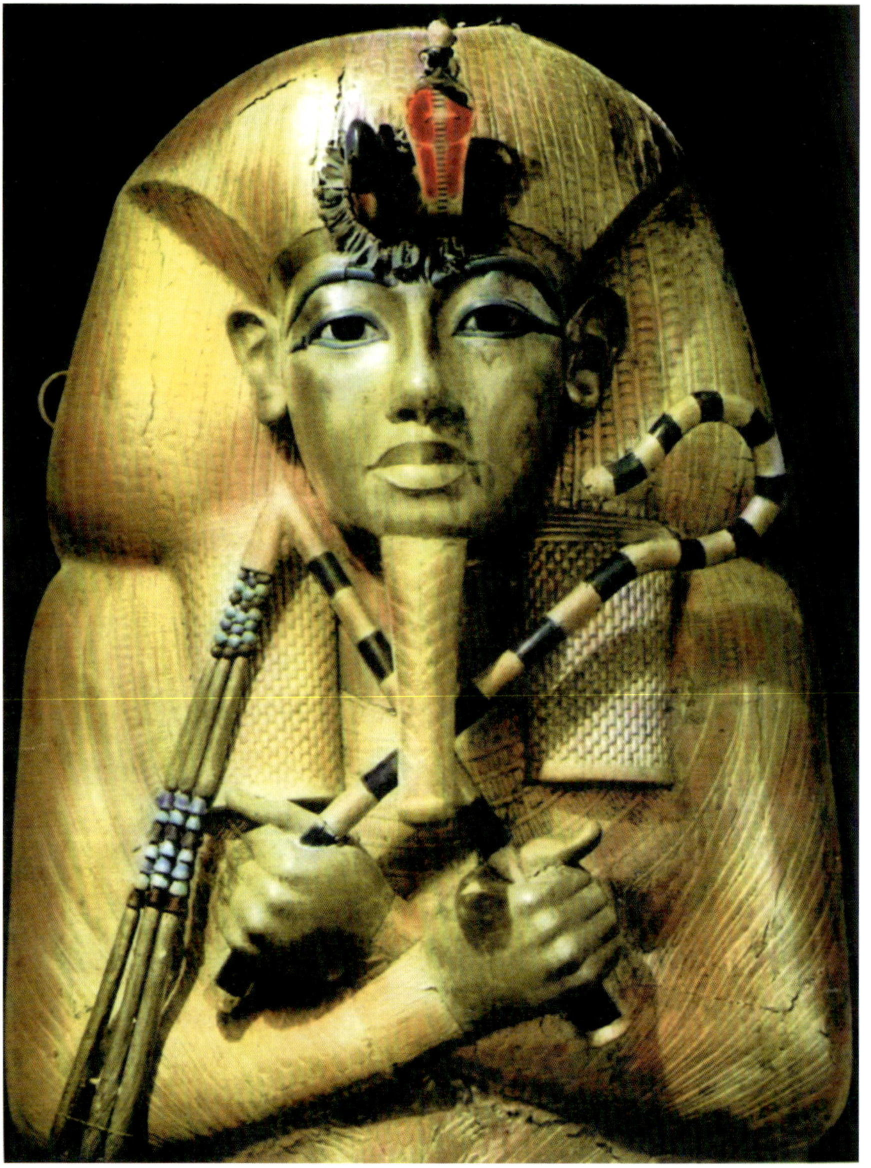

Fig. 44: Part of the first, outermost gilded wooden coffin of Pharaoh Tutankhamun. Black and white photograph, hand-coloured by Howard Carter.

Part III:

The Tomb of Pharaoh Tutankhamun: Images and Texts in its Burial Chamber

1. Overview of the Tomb of Pharaoh Tutankhamun

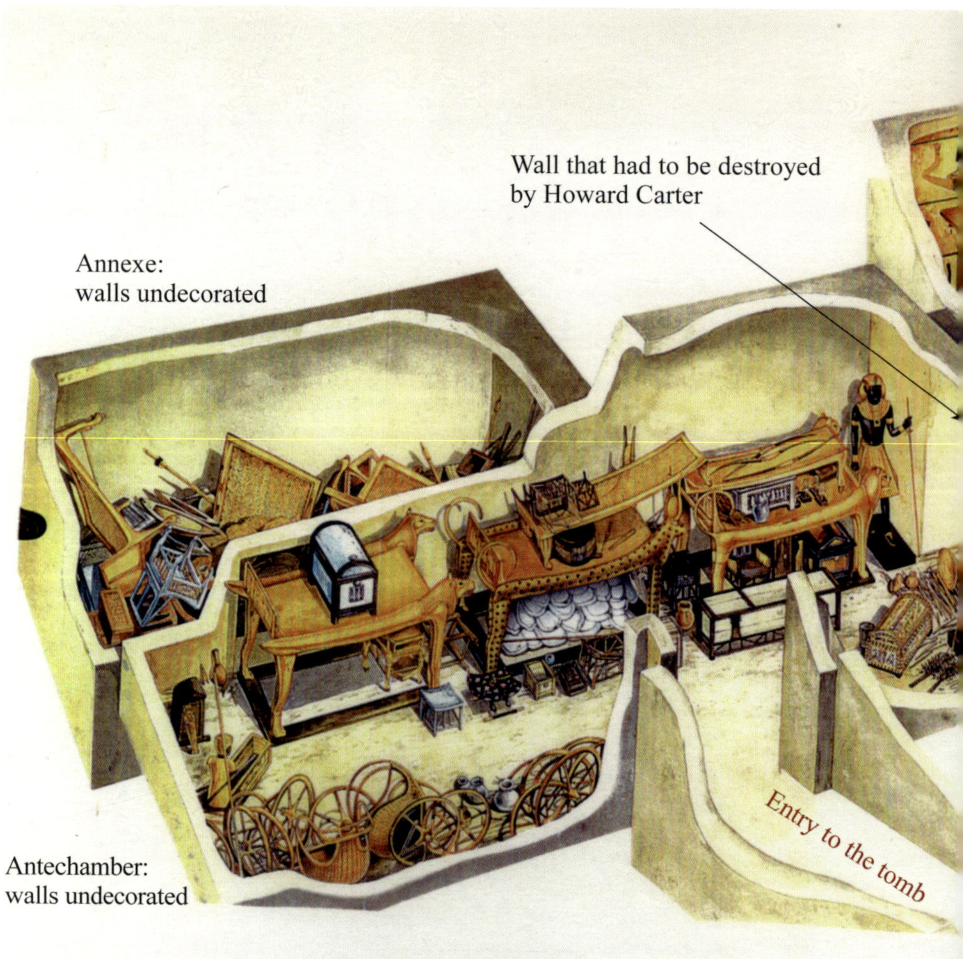

Fig. 45: The tomb of Tutankhamun in the Valley of the Kings remained virtually unplundered. Its discovery by Howard Carter in 1922 was one of the most spectacular archaeological finds of the 20th century, after many years of painstaking searching.

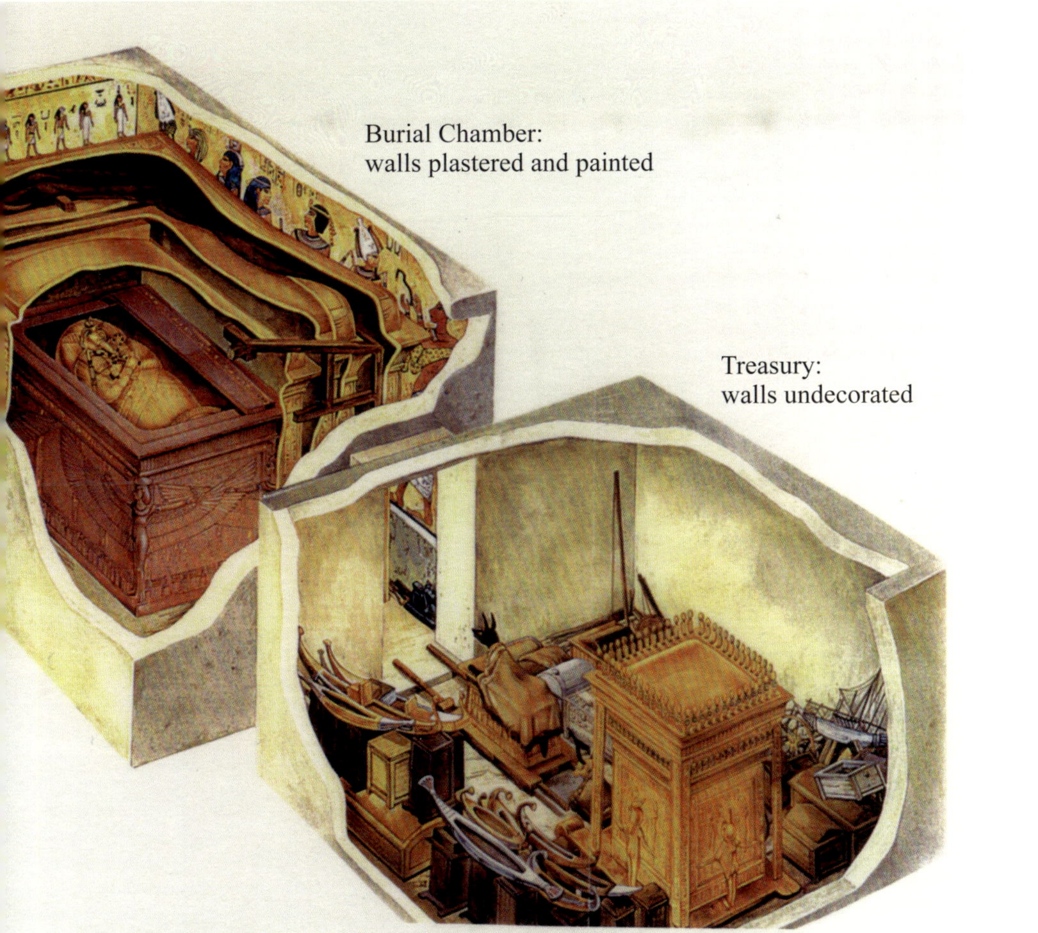

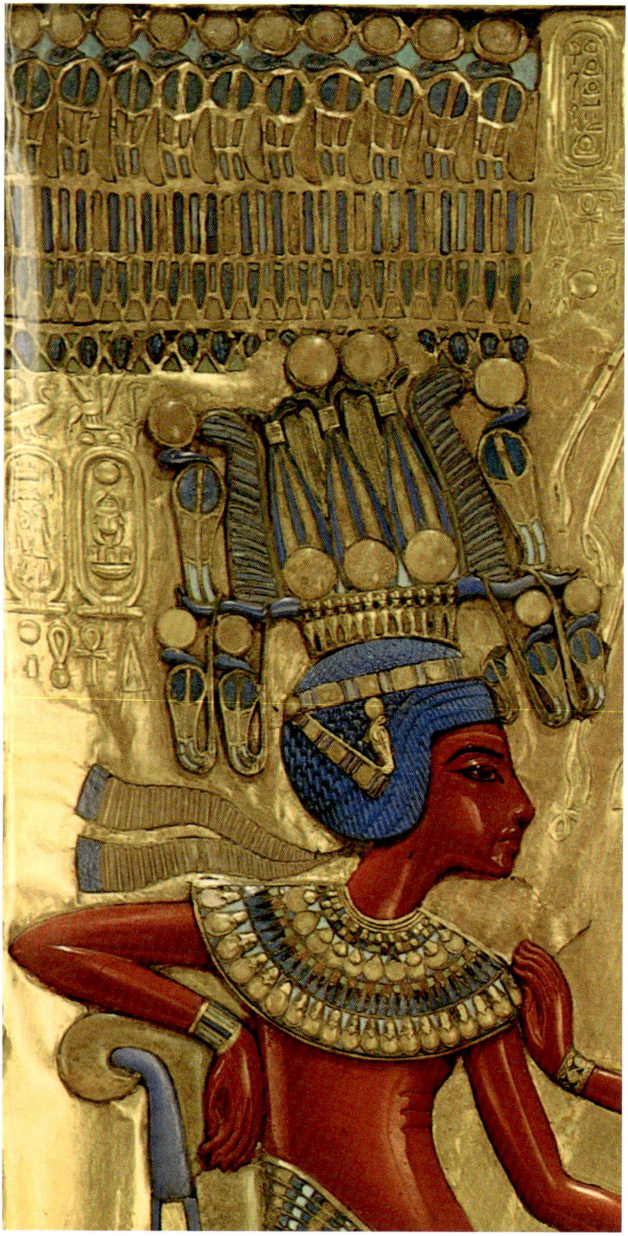

Fig. 46: Tutankhamun in the decoration of the throne found in his tomb (part of fig. 7 on p. 20).

2. Who was Tutankhamun?

Tutankhamun, Pharaoh of the 18th dynasty, ruled from ca. 1332-1323 BCE. He was most probably the son of the heretic Pharaoh Akhenaton. For Tutankhamun's father the god Aton, also represented by the sun-disc, was the only god (as mentioned on p. 21, chapter I.5). Therefore Akhenaton's name shows his intimate relationship to this single god Aton. Likewise, Tutankhamun was given the birthname Tutankhaton, which means «the living image of Aton».

The representations and texts on the golden throne of Tutankhamun, found in his tomb (see fig. 7), show that his wife was Akhenaton's and Nefertiti's third daughter Ankhesenpaaten. However, the names of the royal couple in the inscriptions on this throne were altered to read «Tutankh*amun* and Ankhesen*amun*», reflecting the restoration of the veneration of the god *Amun* and all the other gods and goddesses that were venerated before Akhenaton's revolution.

The examination and analysis of Tutankhamun's mummy revealed that he had died as a teenager. Thus he had become Pharaoh as a child and had reigned for about a decade. During the reign of Tutankhamun the worship of *Aton came to an end*, and extensive restoration was undertaken to repair the damage inflicted on *Amun's* cult during the reign of his father, Pharaoh Akhenaton.

Tutankhamun thus restored the god *Amun* to supremacy. The ban on the cult of *Amun* was lifted and traditional privileges to its priesthood were restored. The capital was moved and the city Akhetaton was abandoned. At that time, Tutankhaton also changed his name to Tutankh*amun*, "Living image of *Amun*".

Tutankhamun's extreme youth leads to the assumption that those moves to restoring the cult of *Amun* were probably initiated by the king's entourage, especially by his vizier and successor Ay (r. 1323-1319 BCE) and his general Horemheb (r. 1319-1292 BCE). They both succeeded Tutankhamun, and must have played major roles in the politics during young Tutankhamun's reign. The cause of Tutankhamun's death is not known, despite repeated but unsubstantiated claims that he had been assassinated. His successor Ay, who survived him by only a few years, honoured his memory, as we will see in the decoration of his tomb.

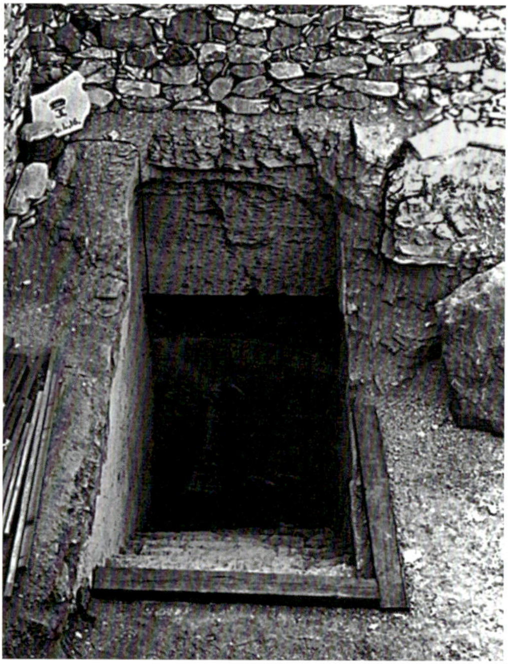

Fig. 47: The stairs leading to the tomb's entrance.

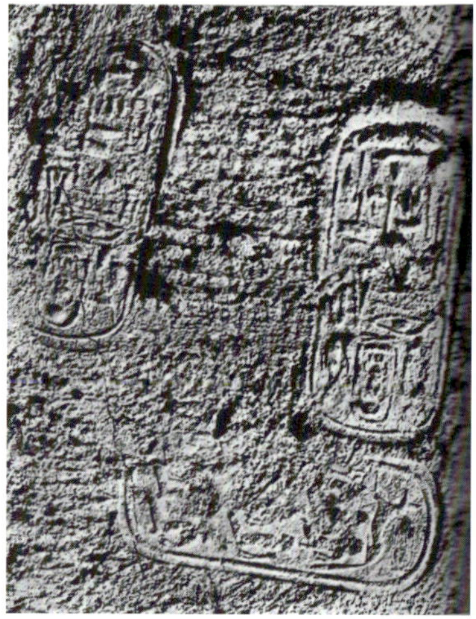

Fig. 48: The intact royal seals, a clear indication that behind it there is still a sealed tomb.

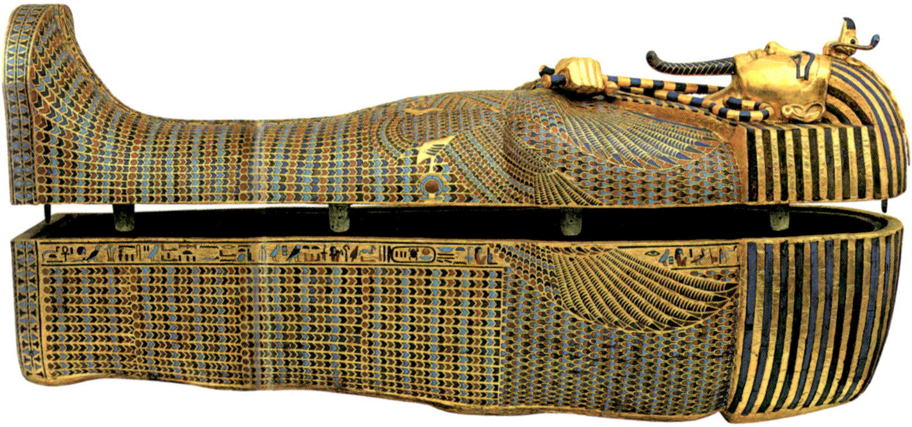

Fig. 49: The second anthropomorphic coffin of Tutankhamun.

3. The Discovery of the Tomb of Tutankhamun

Unlike other Egyptologists of his time, Howard Carter was convinced that the tomb of Tutankhamun could be found somewhere in the vicinity of the tomb of Ramses VI. In the course of seven (!) winter seasons, he excavated without success.

Excavation resumed on November 1st, 1922. Three days later, the remains of ancient huts used during the construction of the tomb of Ramses VI were cleared and, as the workmen removed the final stones, they uncovered a step that had been cut into the valley floor.

By November 5th, 12 descending steps had been exposed (fig. 47). The upper part of a blocked and plastered doorway was revealed. The plaster was impressed with a range of intact oval seals (fig. 48). For Carter, this was a clear indication that he had finally found the still sealed tomb.

Let us read what Carter wrote in his diary: «It was a thrilling moment for an excavator, quite alone save his native staff of workmen, to suddenly find himself, after so many years of toilsome work, on the verge of what looked like a magnificent discovery – an untouched tomb. With certain reluctance I reclosed [the entry to the tomb]. Though I was satisfied that I was on the verge of perhaps a magnificent find, probably one of the missing tombs that I had been seeking for many years, I was much puzzled by the smallness of the opening in comparison with those of other royal tombs in the valley. Its design was certainly of the XVIIIth Dyn. Could it be the tomb of a noble, buried there by royal consent? Or was it a royal cache? As far as my investigations had gone there was absolutely nothing to tell me. Had I known that by digging a few inches deeper I would have exposed seal impressions showing Tût.ankh.Amen's insignia distinctly I would have fervently worked on and set my mind at rest, but as it was, it was getting late, the night had fast set in, the full moon had risen high in the eastern heavens, I refilled the excavation for protection, and with my men selected for the occasion – they like myself delighted beyond all expectation – I returned home and cabled to Ld. C. (Lord Carnarvon then in England) the following message:

"At last have made wonderful discovery in Valley; a magnificent tomb with seals intact; recovered same for your arrival; congratulations."»

On the 23rd of November, after the arrival of Lord Carnarvon, Howard Carter was able to open the still sealed door to the antechamber of the tomb of Tutankhamun. Many weeks of clearing this antechamber were needed before Carter and his team could finally proceed to the opening of the burial chamber.

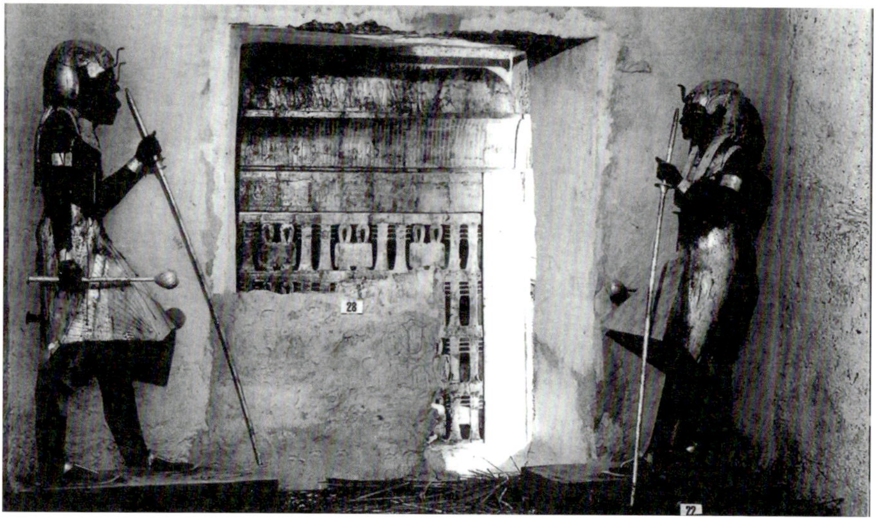

Fig 50: View of the burial chamber after the removal of the bricked-up wall.

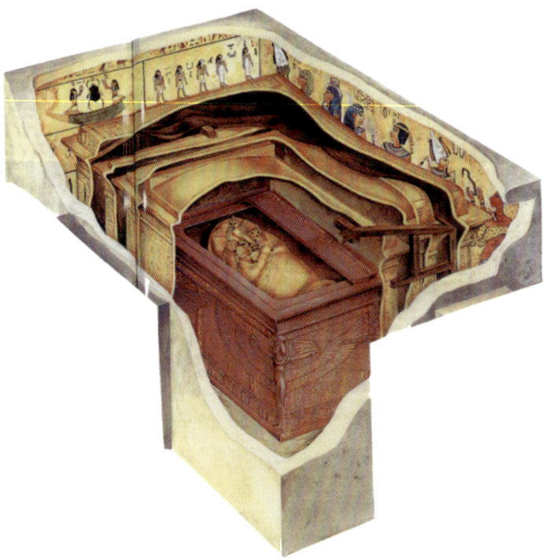

Fig. 51: Close-up view of the burial chamber. Inside this chamber there were four gilded shrines, one inside the other. The innermost one contained the quartzite sarcophagus. Its replica can now also be seen in the facsimile tomb.

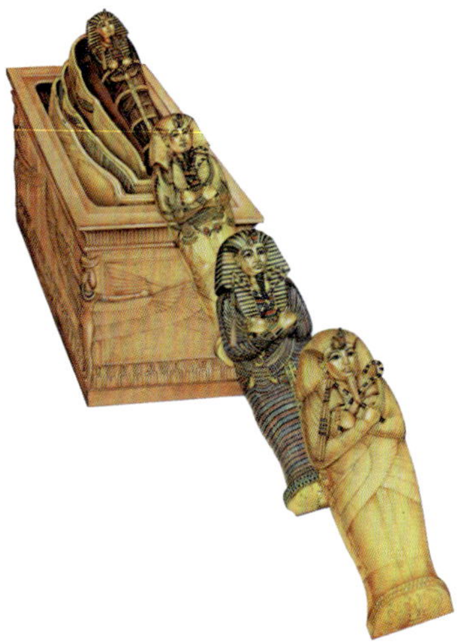

Fig. 52: Inside this sarcophagus, three gilded anthropomorphic coffins had been placed. The last of them contained the mummy with its famous golden mask.

4. The Opening of the Burial Chamber

On February 17th, 1923, Howard Carter had to demolish a bricked up wall that blocked the entrance to the burial chamber (fig. 50). What he then saw was a room almost completely taken up by a huge gilded shrine, leaving only very little space to move between it and the painted wall.

When Carter opened this largest shrine, he discovered inside it another gilded shrine, and then another one, and finally a fourth one, till he arrived at a reddish quartzite sarcophagus, the replica of which can also be seen in the facsimile tomb. Only the largest, outermost shrine had had its seals broken by tomb robbers, who were obviously taken by surprise and had to leave the tomb in haste. The seals of the next two shrines had been left unbroken, while the fourth was not sealed.

Soon after their discovery, these four shrines were moved to the Egyptian Museum in Cairo, where all of them are now on display, together with other treasures from the tomb.

Let us first have a close-up overview of the burial chamber (fig. 51). Its walls are tempera-painted on a yellow gypsum ground, as the burial chamber used to be named *The House of Gold*. Inside the first shrine we can see a section of the three other gilded shrines. The innermost of them contained the reddish quartzite sarcophagus. Inside this sarcophagus three gilded coffins were placed (fig. 52). The last of them contained the mummy with the famous golden mask (see fig. 109).

In the unusually small burial chamber of the tomb of Tutankhamun, the decoration is reduced to a few general scenes. These images can give no more than a summary of the myth of the transition of Osiris-Tutankhamun into the eternal circle of his father, the Sungod Re.

All the religious texts, which were meant to guide the deceased king to his resurrection, and would allow him to move into the eternal circle of the Sungod Re, were *engraved on the four gilded shrines* that covered the quartzite sarcophagus.

An overview of the decoration of these four shrines (after p. 97) will be helpful for a better understanding of the enigmatic idea of the *transformation of Osiris-Tutankhamun to his resurrection as the immortal two-oneness Osiris-Re*.

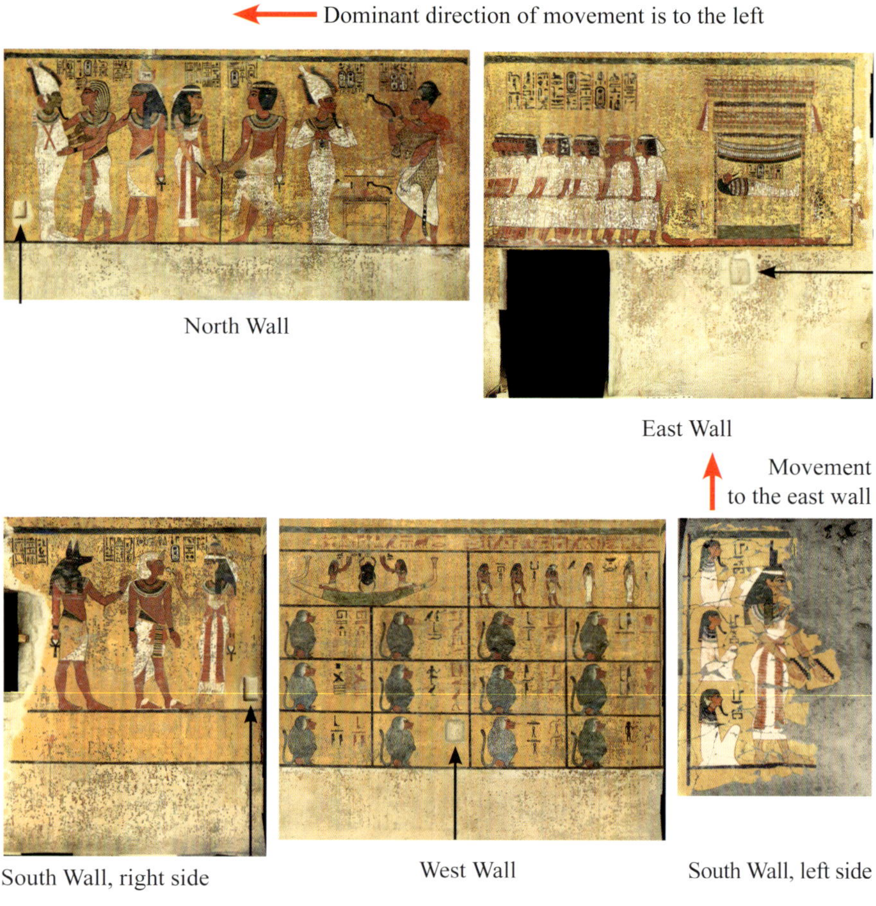

Fig. 53: The four decorated walls of the burial chamber.

On the right side of the south wall, the deceased Pharaoh moves towards the right, towards the west wall depicting the beginning of the Amduat, while *on the left side of the south wall*, the orientation of the Pharaoh (whose picture is missing) is towards the goddess Isis and the east wall, *the place of the new sunrise.*

Inserted in the four walls (see the black arrows ⟶), rectangular niches can be seen, into which magical figurines were placed. In all four directions, they were to protect the deceased from the enemies of Osiris.

5. The Decoration on the Walls, Introduction

The Process of Transformation in Time and as One Image

Today, when we enter a decorated Pharaonic Royal tomb such as that of Pharaoh Tutankhamun, we are taken by surprise. The mysterious images on the walls – gods and goddesses, baboons, scarabs, a human body with a jackal-head – all actually appear to be from another world. Where else but in the landscape of dreams might we find images so alien to our outer-world reality, yet so compelling? Perhaps it is this feature that makes these images remind us unconsciously of an archaic level in our own soul that has largely faded away from the modern enlightened worldview.

In general, the purpose of these images and texts in the royal tombs was to guide the deceased Pharaoh in order to enable him to achieve immortality. In early times, this quest for immortality was only meant for the Pharaoh, but gradually, over the centuries, was also sought by the nobles, and then became a general quest, possible for everybody.

A visit to such a Pharaonic tomb might remind us that the *quest for eternal life has for long been a concern of mankind.* The realisation, that this Pharaonic quest could also have a personal meaning for us today, could motivate us to want to learn more about this culture. The seemingly alien depictions of Pharaonic culture actually reflect the ancient Egyptians' *belief in the potential for the creation of an imperishable centre in each individual* – a belief that is shared by many of the world's religions.

We will start now our observations in the burial chamber of Pharaoh Tutankhamun on the east wall and follow the dominant direction of the movement and orientation of Tutankhamun, going to the left, to the north wall (fig. 53). Next, on the west wall, we see a part of the first hour of the *Amduat*, a royal Book for the Afterlife. This scene has to be seen together with the introduction scene on the south wall (right side), where the dead king is introduced to the Netherworld in order to join his father, the Sungod Re in his barque for his rejuvenation. Finally, we look at the destroyed part of the south wall. There, on the fragmented parts of the left part of the wall, we see the goddess Isis, *who finally welcomes the deceased Pharaoh, her husband and son Osiris-Tutankhamun, to his resurrection* (this part has been destroyed).

6. The east Wall

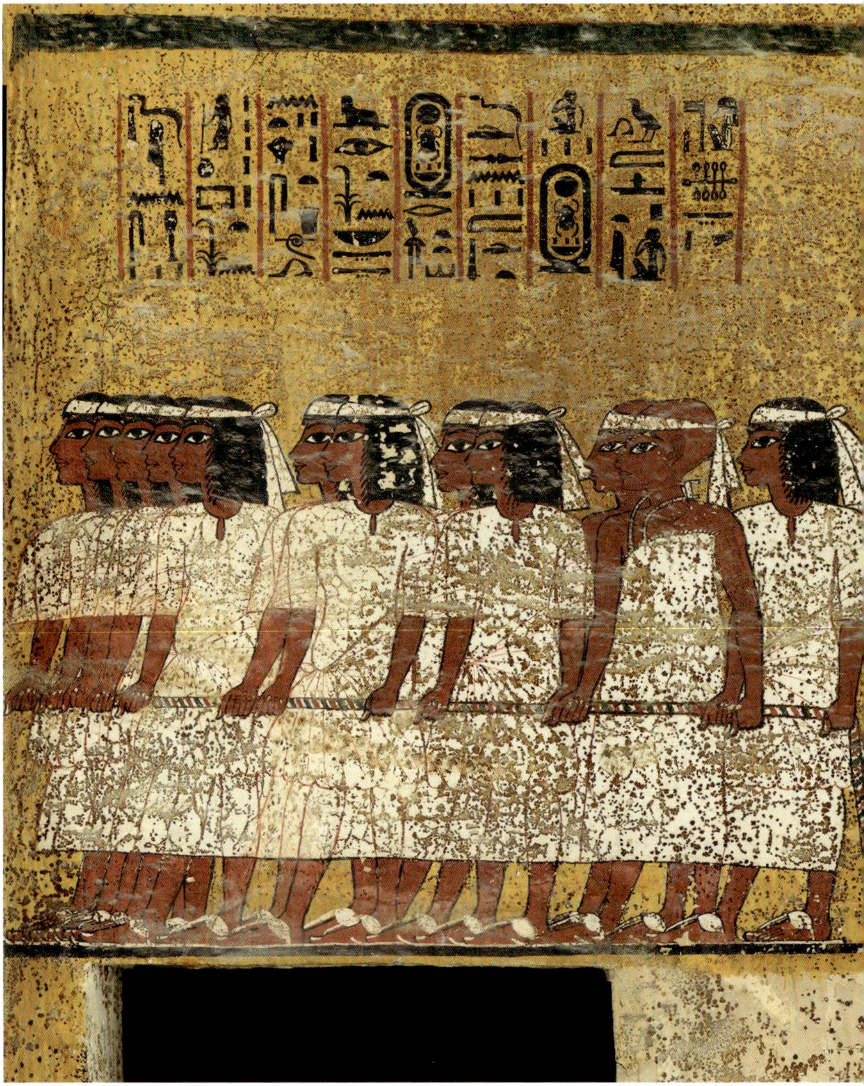

Fig. 54: The east wall.

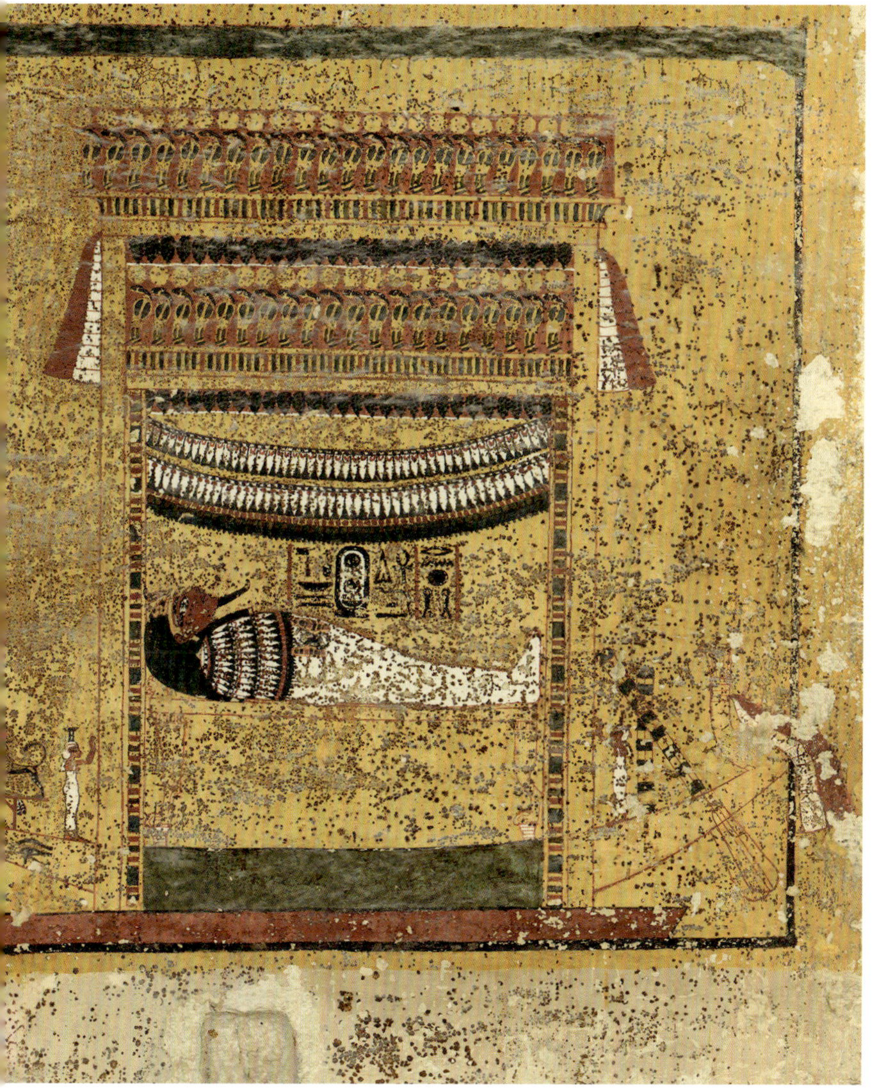

This wall shows the funeral procession, a scene that is usually only found in private tombs. On top of the scene we find the hieroglyph 𓇯 for heaven, pointing to the cosmic dimension of the process that is now taking place.

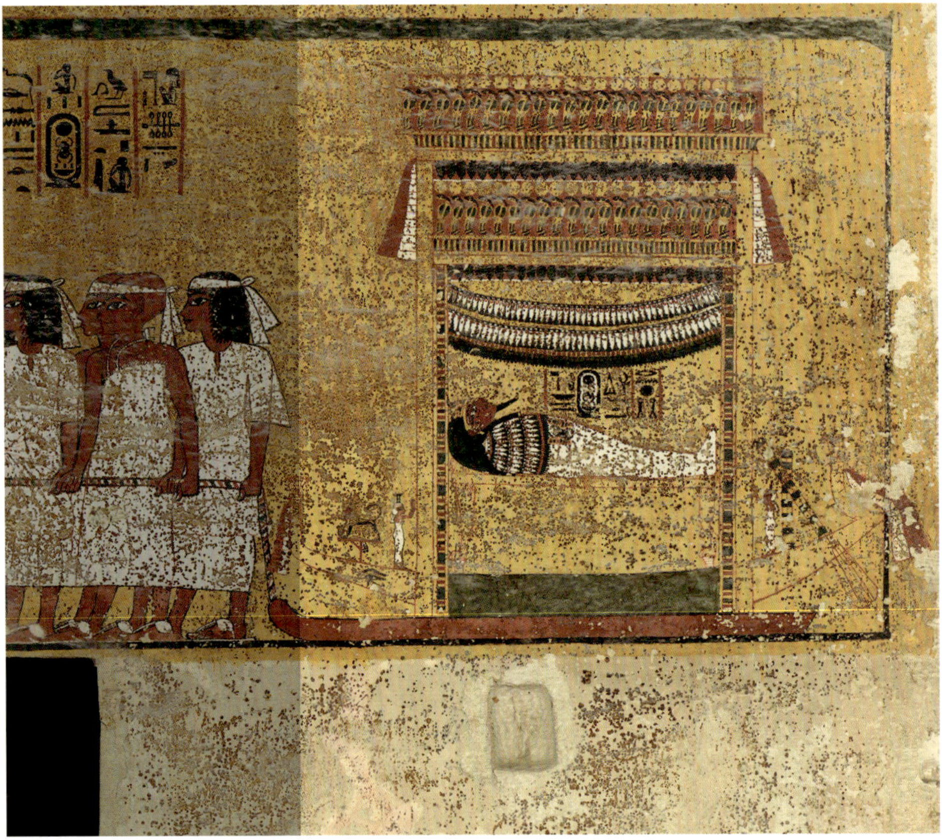

Fig. 55: The east wall, right side.

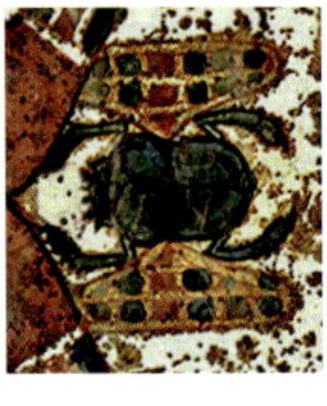

Fig. 56: Enlarged part of the mummy of Tutankhamun, showing the black-winged scarab, however with no sun-disc between his forelegs yet.

6a. The east Wall, right Side

Here we see the mummy of the Pharaoh placed on a barely visible lion-shaped bier (fig. 57). The mummy

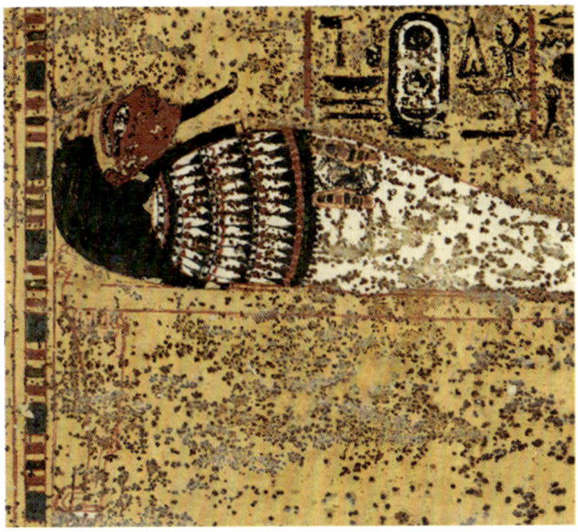

Fig. 57: Enlarged part of the mummy on the barely visible lion-shaped bier.

is covered with a mask, having an *uraeus*-serpent (cobra with raised head) on its head and the curved beard of a god. This depiction resembles the famous golden mask of Tutankhamun (see fig. 109). The text above the mummified dead Pharaoh, written above him in hieroglyphs, reads: *«The perfect god, master of the two-lands, Neb-kheperu-re* (throne name of Tutankhamun, see glossary), *living eternally and forever.»*

A black scarab with coloured wings, symbol of the rejuvenated Sungod when he rises in the morning, is placed above his chest as part of a pectoral (fig. 56).

The lion-shaped bier with the mummy on it, is placed in a high shrine that is protected on top by a row of 20 *uraeus*-serpents, symbols for rejuvenation. A row of blue grapes is shown below them. Above this shrine there is another shrine that is also protected on top by a row of 23 *uraeus*-serpents and a row of grapes below. In a subtle way, this second shrine is superimposed on the first one, thus giving the impression of there being only one shrine. The lion-shaped bier with these two shrines is laid on a boat which used to be the method of transportation of the Sungod through the night, to enable him to overcome his death by this night-journey, rising in the morning as the rejuvenated Sungod. The barque with its two shrines is placed on a sledge which is pulled by a team of twelve officials. At the head of the mummy we see a small representation of the goddess Nephthys (see fig. 58), while at the other end of the barque, at the feet of the mummy, we see her sister Isis. These two sisters, each dressed in a white garment, are wearing white wigs, and, with uplifted arms, are mourning the dead Osiris.

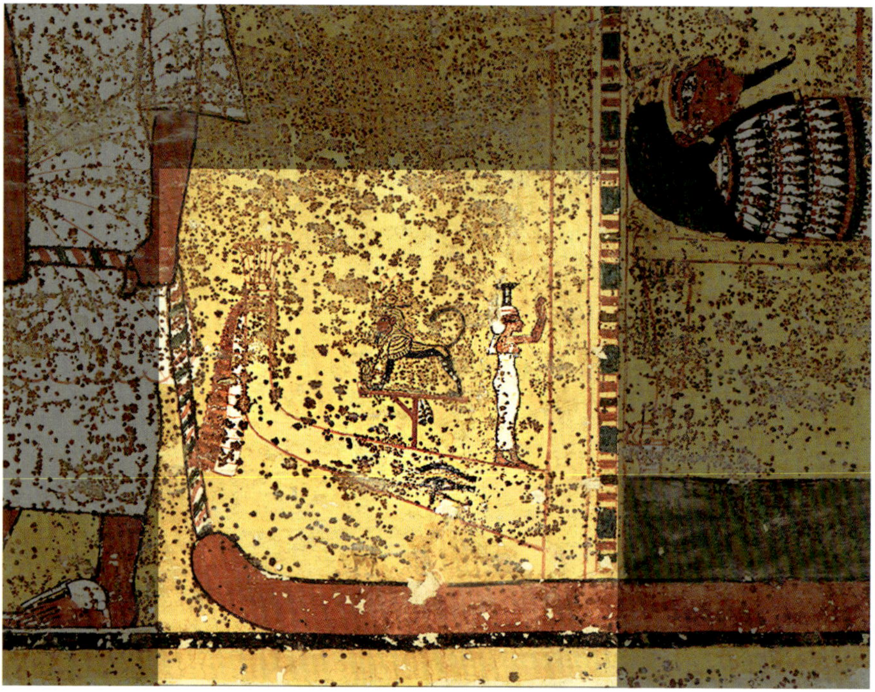

Fig. 58: Detail of the east wall, right side, with the goddess Nephthys.

Detail: The east Wall, right Side

We see the goddess Nephthys standing on the barque in a white dress (fig. 58). Compared to the pictures of goddesses in pre-Amarna time and after Tutankhamun, this goddess, and her sister Isis on the other side of the shrine, are surprisingly small. This may indicate a kind of tentative revival of their representation, which had been totally forbidden during the reign of Tutankhamuns`s father.

Between Nephthys and the prow of the barque, we see a sphinx on top of a stand: the head of the dead Pharaoh with the body of a lion (fig. 59). An *udjat*-eye, painted below on the prow of the barque, is a protective symbol for the funerary barques. Such eyes can still be seen on ships of today on the river Nile.

All the scenes in this burial chamber are covered with brown spots: they were caused by a fungus that had probably been introduced and started to spread at the time of the burial of Tutankhamun. This fungus was then nourished by the humidity from the fresh plaster and paint used in the period before the closing of the tomb.

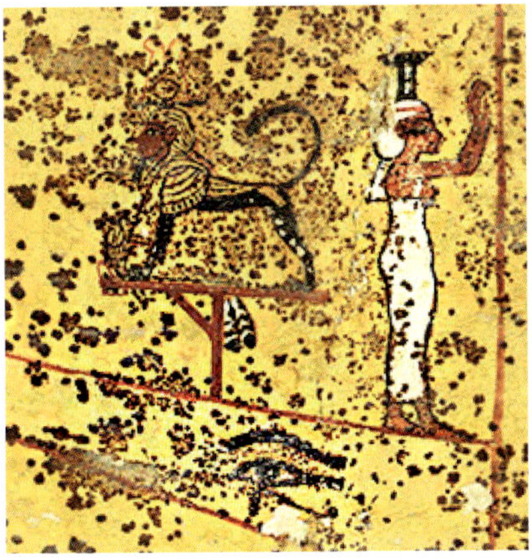

Fig. 59: Detail of the east wall, right side: the stand with the sphinx and the *udjat*-eye below.

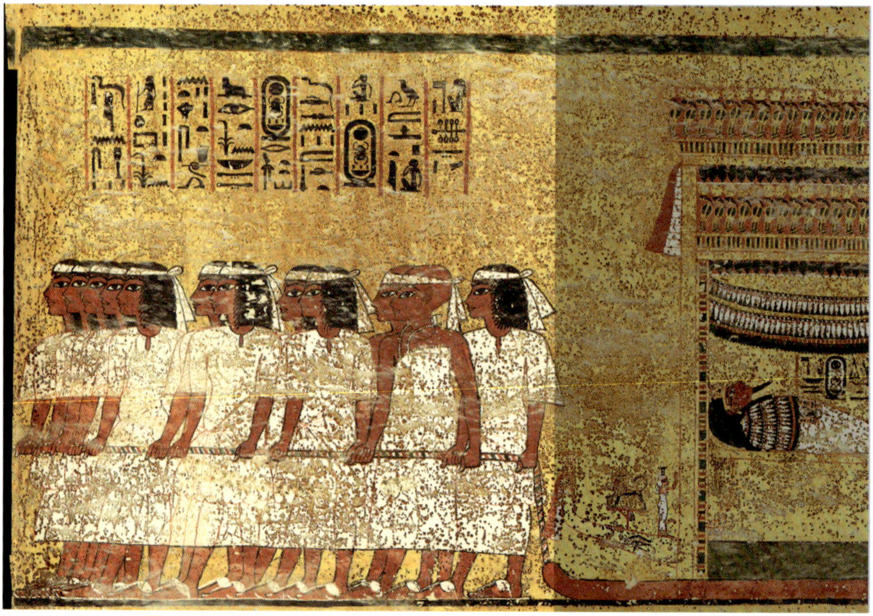

Fig. 60: The east wall, left side.

6b. The east Wall, left Side

Twelve men, wearing white sandals, pull the sledge with the mummy of the deceased Pharaoh. This shows that the scene on the east wall is taking place in our world. It depicts a typical funerary procession. The twelve men are represented in five groups. A group of five is shown at the front, followed by three pairs of men and finally one single man. All men, except those two in front of the single one, are depicted identically, with a white garment. Their black wigs are adorned with the typical white ribbon of mourning. The two men in front of the single man wear the ribbon of mourning on a shaven skull. Their tunics have the characteristic shoulder straps of a vizier, indicating that they are the two viziers of Upper and Lower Egypt. The last person, standing alone and closest to the mummy, may well be the general Horemheb, who became Tutankhamun's successor after Ay.

The text above the twelve men is given here as an example of hieroglyphic writing. The text must be read from the top down, starting from the left.

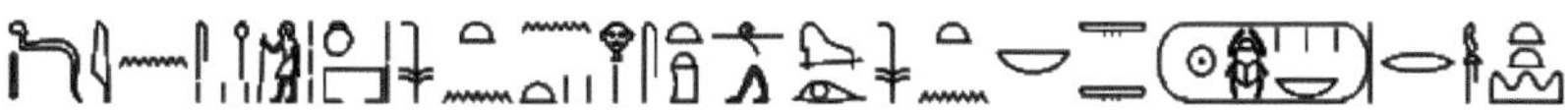

ḏd-mdw jn smrw nw pr-nswt ntj ḥr stꜣ Wsjr nswt nb tꜣwj Nb-ḫprw-Rꜥ r jmntt

Words spoken by the officials of the State who are towing Osiris, King of the Two Lands, Neb-kheperu-re (Tutankhamun's throne name)*, to the West.*

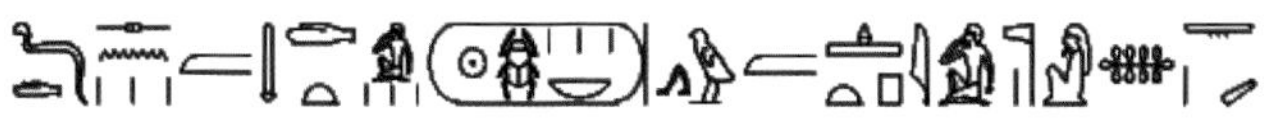

ḏd.sn m mdwt Nb-ḫprw-Rꜥ jw m ḥtp j nṯr sꜣ-tꜣ

They say the words: «Come, O Neb-kheperu-re (Tutankhamun)*, come in peace, o god, protector of the land!»*

7. The north Wall

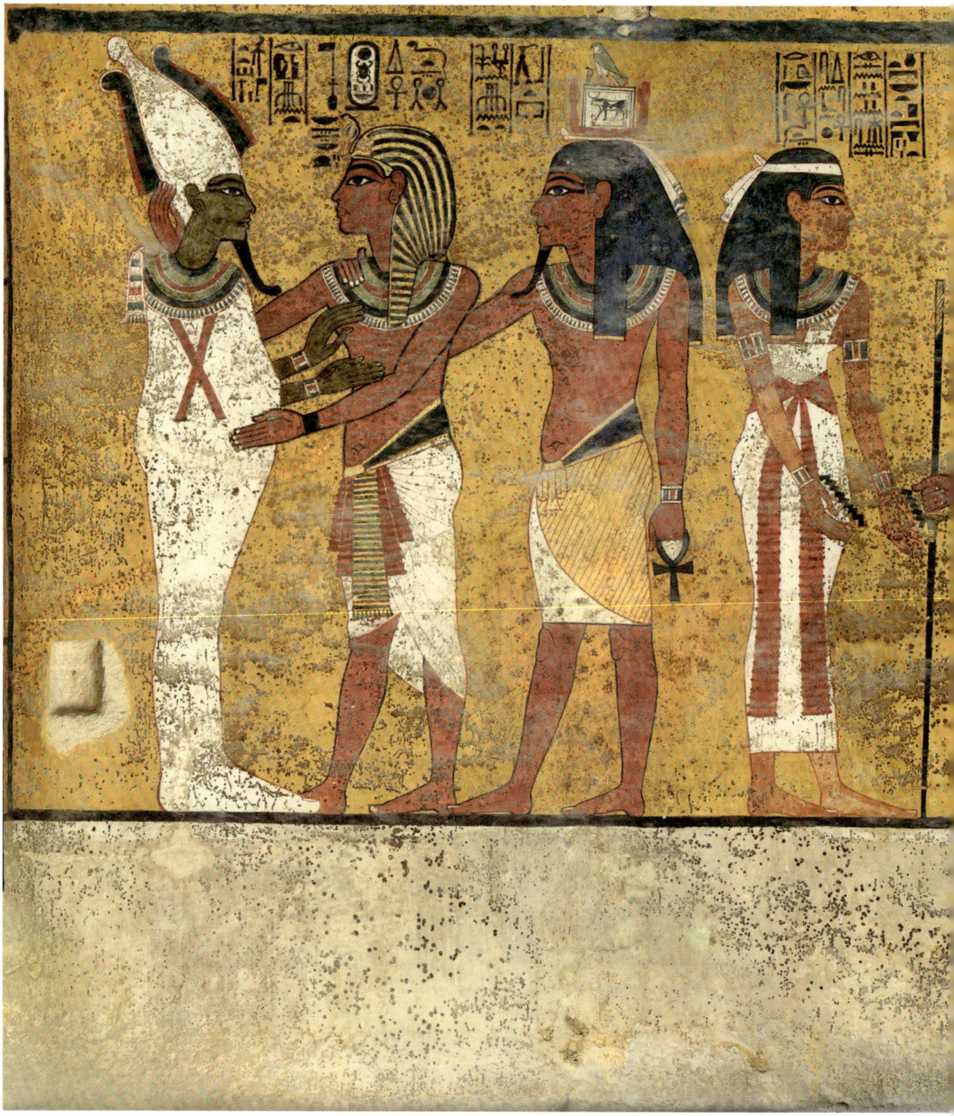

Fig. 61: The north wall.

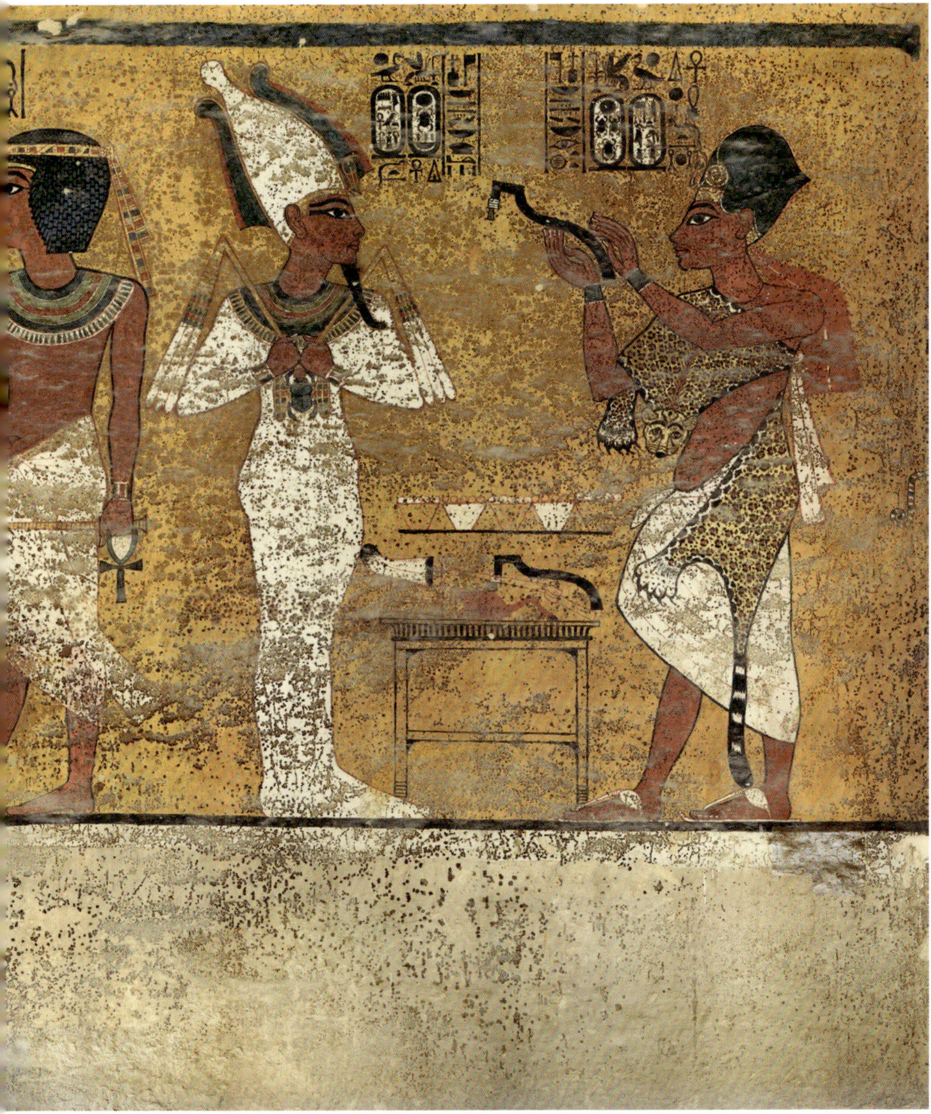

All along the top of the whole wall we find the hieroglyph 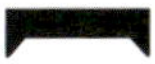 for heaven.

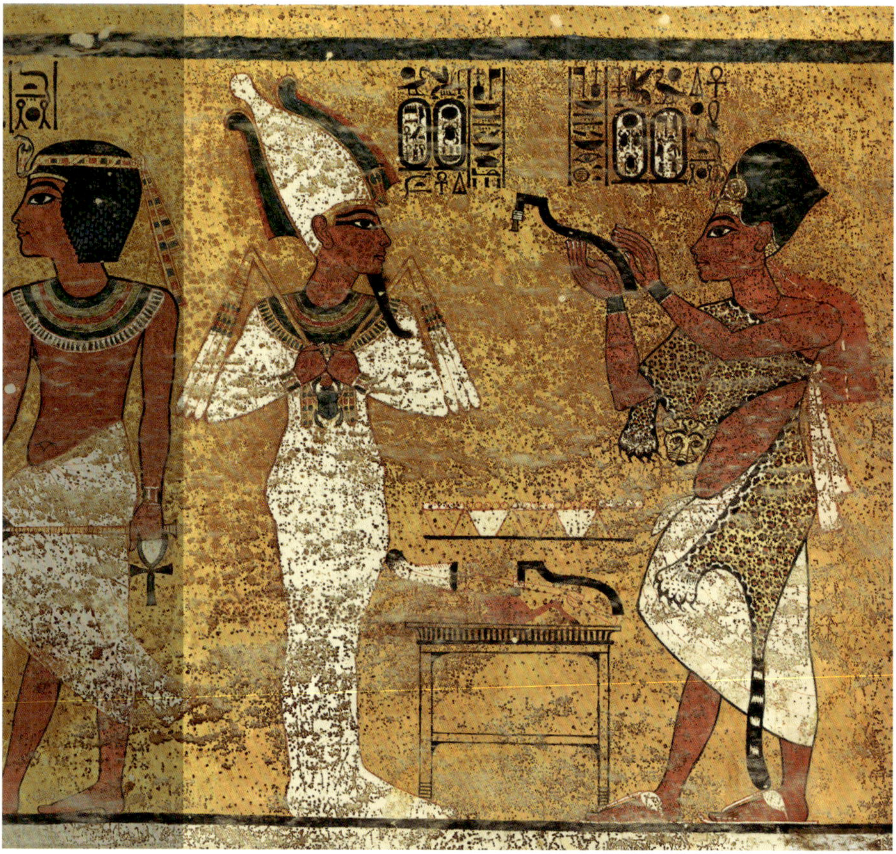

Fig. 62: The north wall, 1st scene.

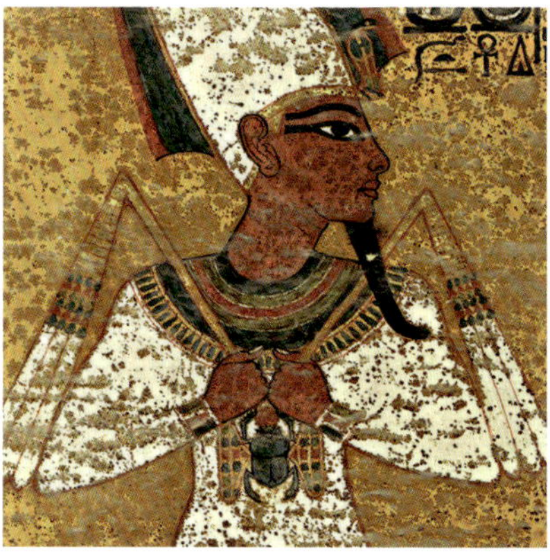

Fig. 63: Enlarged detail of Tutankhamun as Osiris with a necklace. On it we see a green, winged scarab that carries the sun-disc between his forelegs, symbol for his forthcoming resurrection.

7a. North Wall, 1st Scene

In royal tombs, this scene is unique: To the right, we see the new succeeding Pharaoh Ay, who is named in the hieroglyphic text above him. He performs the ritual of the "Opening of the Mouth" on his 'father' Tutankhamun, although Ay is quite older than the deceased Pharaoh. The new king Ay is depicted as youthful, being a little smaller than the dead Tutankhamun. Ay is dressed in the leopard skin of the *sem*-priest, wearing, as the only royal emblem, the blue crown with the *uraeus*-serpent. He has white sandals on his feet, showing that he performs this ritual in our world. As successor of the deceased Pharaoh, he performs the role that is usually reserved for the eldest son of the deceased king. This ritual establishes the legitimacy of his right to the throne.

The text above Ay reads:

«The good god, Master of the Two-lands, Master of rituals, King of Upper and Lower Egypt, god's father, Ay (kheper-kheperu-re), Son of Re, Tutankhamun, endowed eternally with life and forever like Re.»

The dead Tutankhamun is not represented as a mummy, as is usually the case for the ritual of the "Opening of the Mouth". Instead he is depicted in the form of Osiris with the *atef*-crown. This is a white crown with two ostrich feathers on each side. On its front there is an *uraeus*-serpent. His beard, with the curved tip, indicates his divine status.

Unlike the green-skinned Osiris that we see to the far left of the north wall, the skin of the dead Tutankhamun is similar to the skin of "his son" Ay. In his hands, as they emerge from the wrapping, he carries two identical flails, emblems of his power. Around his neck we see a large necklace from which hangs a green winged scarab (here with a sun-disc), the mysterious insect-energy, which, according to ancient Egyptian belief, pushes the sun across the horizon to its rebirth (fig. 63).

The text above Osiris-Tutankhamun reads: *«The good god, Lord of the Two-lands, Lord of the Crowns, King of Upper and Lower Egypt Neb-kheperu-re, son of Re, Tutankhamun, Master of the Heliopolis of the South (= Thebes), endowed with life, eternally.»*

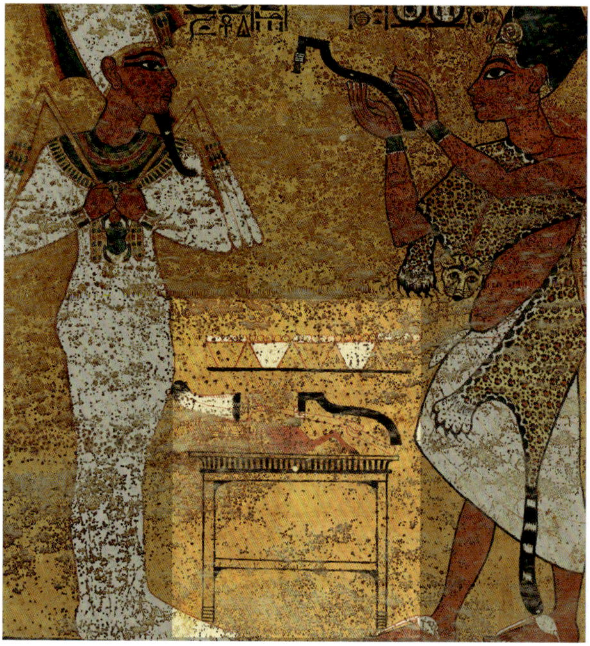

Fig. 64: Detail of north wall, 1st scene: table with the utensils for the ritual of the "Opening of the Mouth" on the mummy of Tutankhamun.

Let us look at what happened to a deceased person in Ancient Egypt before he/she was buried.

The mummification ritual:

The embalming process included a bathing of the corpse in a liquid, containing salt natron. This word natron comes from the Egyptian word *netjer* which means god. By soaking the corpse in 'god-liquid', it was, so to speak, deified and immortalised. Step by step, the corpse was transformed into the shape of 'eternal' matter. This immortalisation was simultaneously regarded as a complete regeneration of the deceased: a rebirth, not out of the womb of a mortal woman, but out of the primordial waters of *Nun*. After having been soaked completely and even having been partly dissected, like Osiris, the deceased is thought to resurrect out from the depth of waters of *Nun*. Thus also the dead Tutankhamun became first Osiris-Tutankhamun.

In a second part, as we will learn from the text and pictures in the tomb of Tutankhamun, this Osiris-Tutankhamun will be gradually transformed, so as to be able to join his father, the Sungod Re, thus turnig into Re-Osiris.

Detail: The Utensils for the Ritual of the "Opening of the Mouth"

The detail of the 1st scene, given on the left side, shows the table with the utensils used by the designated new Pharaoh Ay. They are needed to perform the ritual of the "Opening of the Mouth" for his deceased 'father' Tutankhamun, who is represented, as we saw on the page before, as the god Osiris.

The ritual of the "Opening of the Mouth" was a symbolic animation of the mummy by magically opening its mouth so that it could breathe, speak and also see. It involved a great number of episodes.

Different tools that were used to perform the ceremony are seen in fig. 64, such as a ritual arm-shaped censer, a spooned blade, a serpent-head blade, a calf's leg, a magic human finger and a variety of other utensils. The small vases on top contain incense.

The ancient Egyptians believed that in order for a person's body and soul to survive in the afterlife, it would need to have food and water. The ritual of the "Opening of the Mouth" was thus also performed in order that the person who had died and been mummified, could eat and drink again in thc afterlife.

Today we can understand the death of 'father' Tutankhamun as the end of a way of ruling the state. In the period that follows the death of a king, there is first of all a period of grief and mourning, but it is also a time of uncertainty and disorientation.

By representing this ritual of the "Opening of the Mouth" done by the designated new Pharaoh, the forthcoming new king, a magical act is performed. This scene inside a Pharaonic tomb – which is unknown in other royal tombs – was meant to help the emerging of the renewed general attitude: *The consolidation of the restoration of the cult of Amun and all the other abandoned deities*.

The ritual of the "Opening of the Mouth" is a symbolic act that allows the spirit of Osiris-Tutankhamun to speak, see and live again. In this way, his spirit can manifest itself anew and be alive for the humans on earth. This is a guarantee for a living relationship between this the world of the living and Osiris-Tutankhamun, and hence to the realm of the dead, and in this way to the gods and all the ancestors, known today as the world of the unconscious.

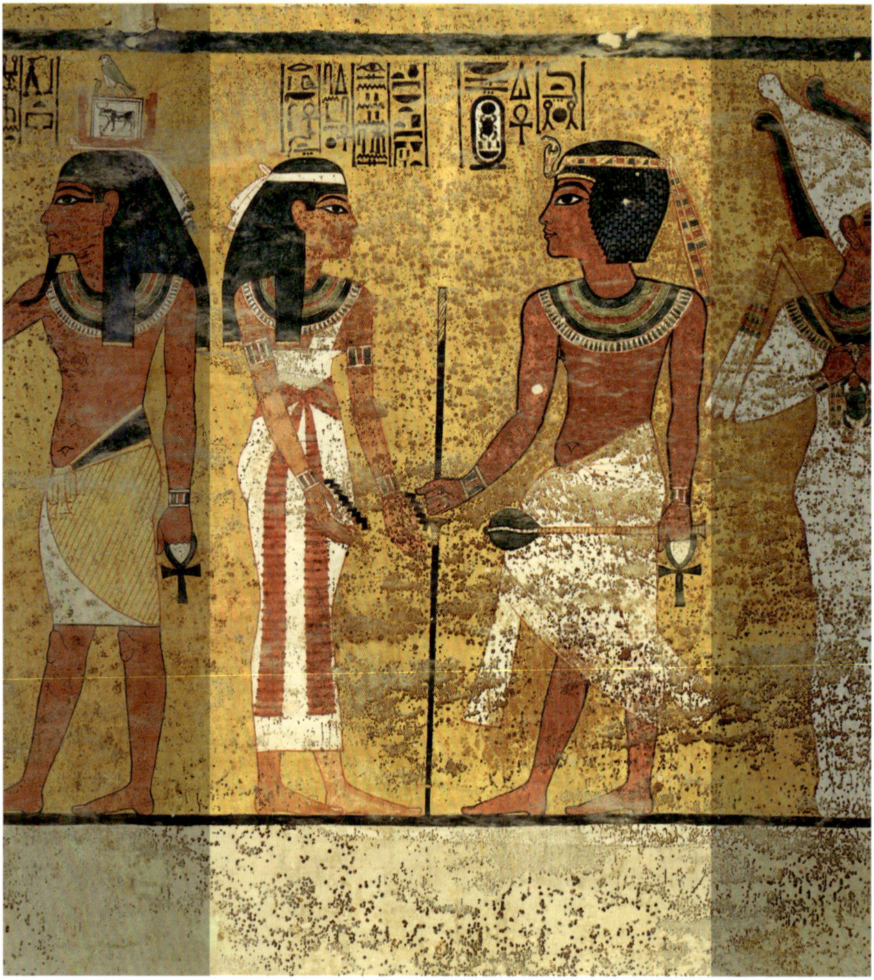

Fig. 65: Detail of north wall, 2nd scene.

7b. North Wall, 2nd scene

To the right of this scene we see the Pharaoh Tutankhamun, presented as a simply dressed human being and barefoot, indicating that he is in the Beyond. Only the *ankh*-sign of life as well as the staff in his hands and the *uraeus*-serpent on his forehead denote his royal status. This is different from the scene before, where we saw Tutankhamun as the god Osiris. The hieroglyphs above him read: «*The Ruler of the Two-lands Neb-kheperu-re, endowed with life eternally and forever.*»

On Tutankhamun's left, we see the goddess Nut, who welcomes the Pharaoh. In her outstretched hands are two hieroglyphs 𓈖 for water, which the Egyptians name *nini*, meaning «to me to me». The sign of water will connect the goddesss Nut with the deceased from this, our world.

Nut is wearing a tight-fitting dress with a large red linen belt around her hips. She wears jewels, a pectoral and bracelets. Around her wig she wears the white ribbon of mourning. The text reads: «*Nut, Mistress of the Sky, Lady of the Gods, she makes nini to the one to whom she has given birth, she gives health and life to your nose, with the result that you live forever.*»

In the morning, the mother goddess Nut was thought to give birth to her son, the Sungod Re. In the evening, she receives the dying Sungod again. The Pharaoh, who is the son of Re, is here received by the Mistress of the Sky, Nut, who is named in the text as the mother of the deceased. In this way, the Pharaoh Tutankhamun is identified with the Sungod. Nut invites the deceased into her realm of the Beyond. In this way the death of Tutankhamun means the return of the son to the womb of his mother. This can also be seen in many sarcophagi of Pharaonic Egypt, where – on the inside of the sarcophagus' lid – an image of the goddess Nut takes the deceased into her arms.

This 2nd scene in the middle of the north wall, could point to the central importance of the coming together of the deceased Pharaoh with the Mistress of the Sky, *the son with his mother Nut.*

As the Pharaoh Tutankhamun now continues to live forever, his people on earth have also a guarantee for life and a connection to the Beyond, and in this way also to the divine animal world, symbolised by the *uraeus*-serpent on the head of Tutankhamun.

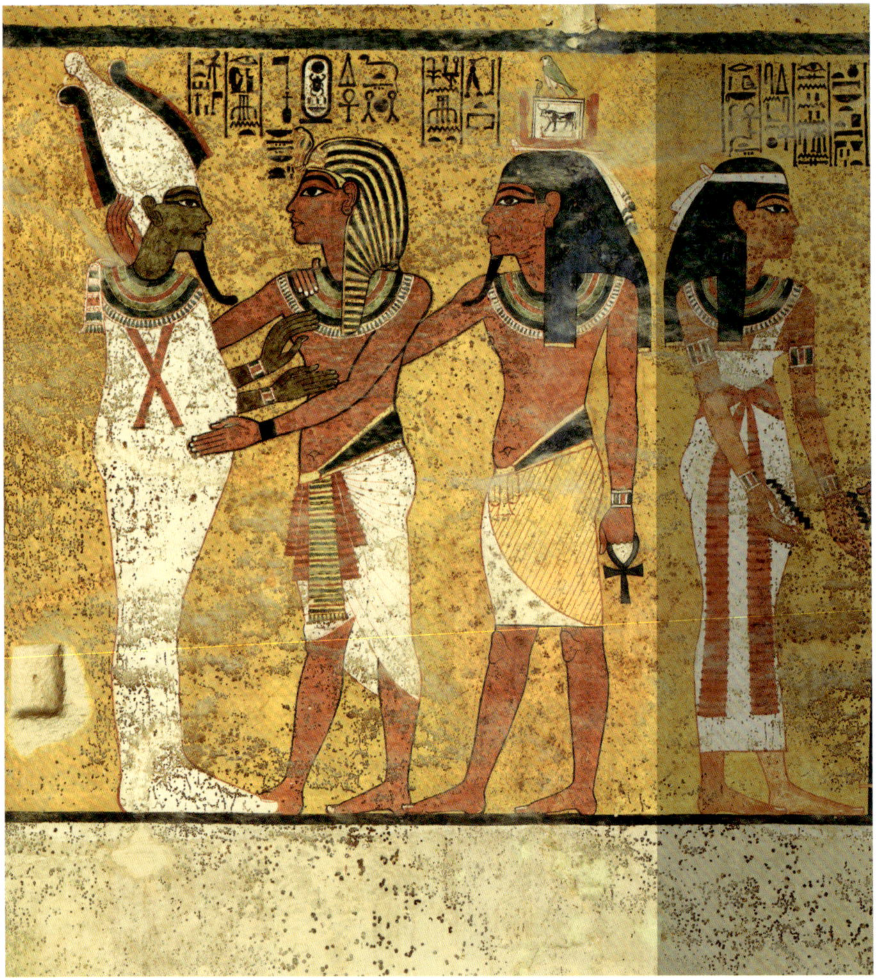

Fig. 66: Detail of north wall, 3rd scene.

7c. North Wall, 3rd scene

This scene shows three figures: In the centre we see the king again without sandals, indicating that he is in the Beyond. Behind the king is his *Ka*. Man is born with his *Ka*, that is his vital energy. After death, he unites with his *Ka*, as it is said in Egyptian language "to die" = "to pass to one's *Ka*". The head of the *Ka* is covered with a wig, on top of which we see the 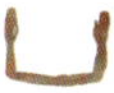 *Ka*-hieroglyph. It surrounds two hieroglyphs 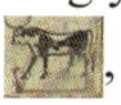, signifying *«powerful bull»*, an attribute for the king. The *Ka* has the long curved beard of the gods in the Beyond. In one hand, he holds the sign of life, and the other he places on the back of the young king, who stands in front of him. This gesture can be understood as signifying protection, or introduction to Osiris. A short text defines him as *«The royal Ka of the one who is at the head of the royal palace»*.

Tutankhamun is depicted in the mode of the living, wearing a striped *nemes*-headcloth. It is familiar to us from the golden mask of Tutankhamun and is a sign of the Pharaoh's power. But the Pharaoh does not yet have the curved beard of the gods. The fact that Tutankhamun is once more presented, as in the 2nd scene, barefoot and clad only in a loincloth, with a hair-cloth from which there emerges an uraeus-serpent and a necklace, denotes his royal status *and* his human nature.

The king embraces *«Osiris, the Foremost of the West, the good god»*, who receives him, as can be seen by the two hands protruding from the mummy. Osiris wears the *atef*-crown, the white crown with two ostrich feathers on each side, but without an *uraeus*-serpent. His flesh is green, like the vegetation which, in Egypt, is born again after the flooding of the Nile. From his mummified body, Osiris extends his two arms, which touch the body of Tutankhamun. This in fact touches us as well, we who are today privileged to see these scenes, which were never meant to be seen by mortal beings. Perhaps it is important for us to learn once again from our Pharaonic ancestors about the reality of the Beyond, and about how we can live with this other reality. This last scene on the North wall represents the union of the deceased Pharaoh – together with his *Ka*-power – with Osiris, the Foremost of the Netherworld. This can be understood as *a renewed connection of the human realm with the reality of the Beyond.*

8. The south Wall

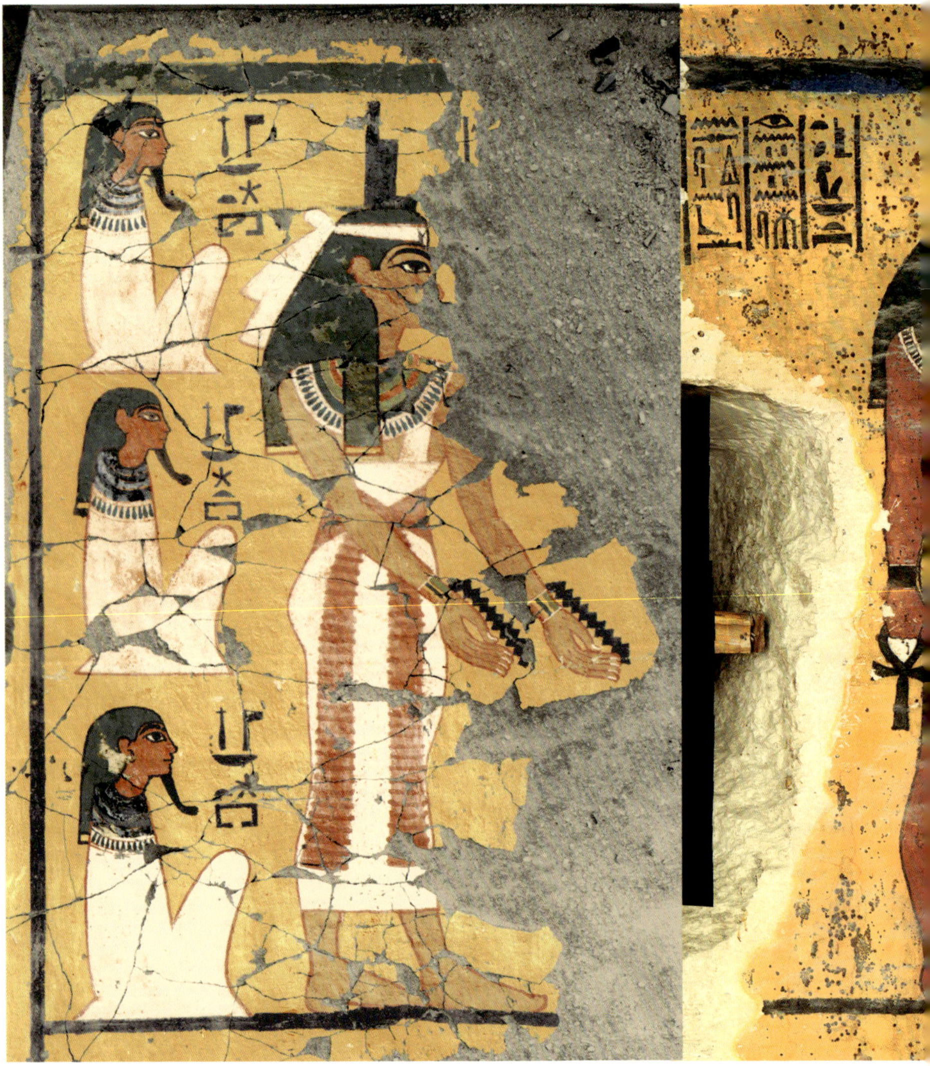

Fig. 67: The reconstructed south wall.

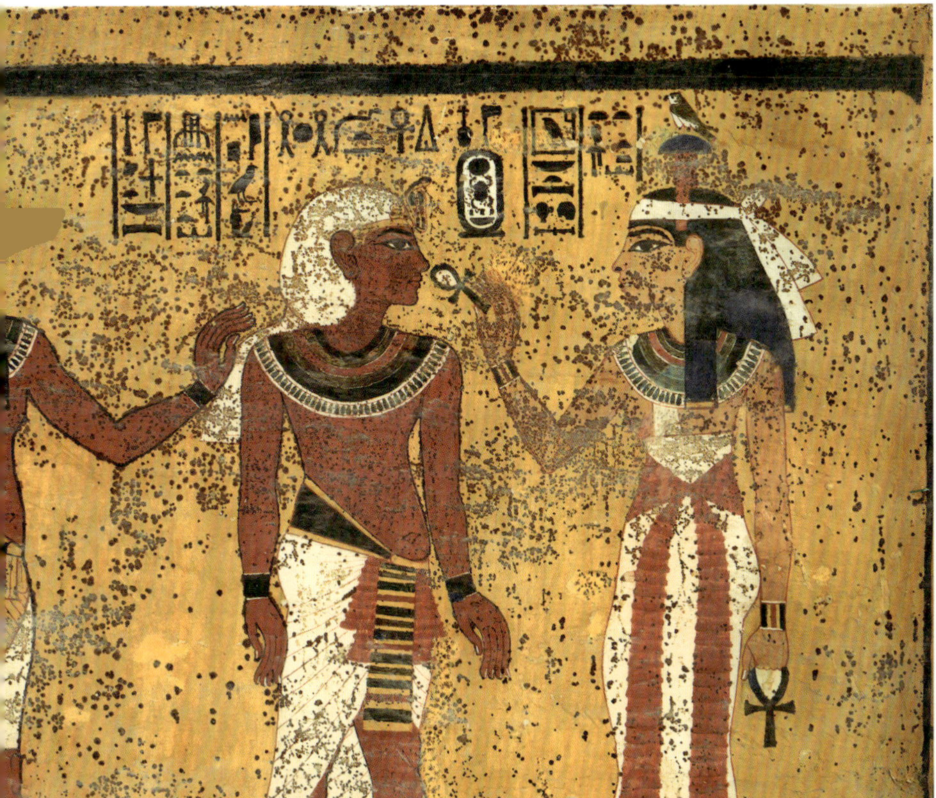

All along the top of the wall, we find again the hieroglyph 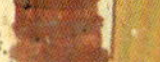 for heaven.

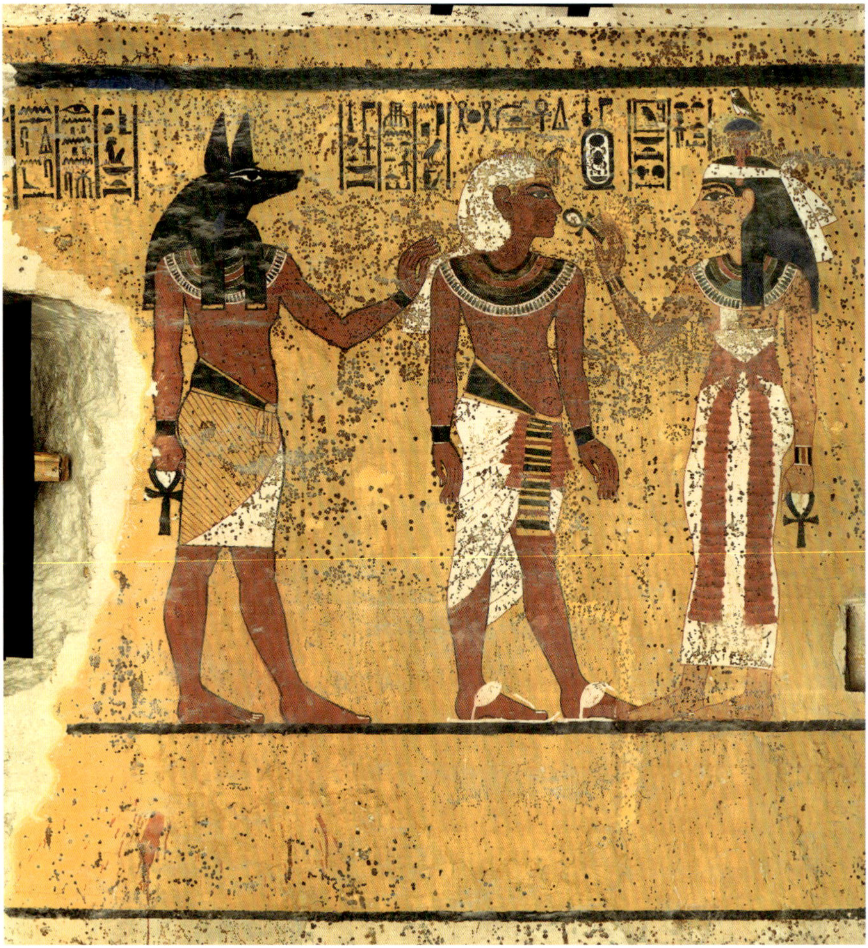

Fig. 68: Detail of south wall, right part.

8a. South Wall, right Part that leads to the west Wall

To the right of this south wall we see the goddess Hathor (fig. 68). Again she is named *Mistress of the Sky*, and she, too, is clothed in the same way as the goddess Nut in the centre of the north wall. On her head, inserted into a white ribbon, she has the hieroglyph of the West, thereby indicating that she is the goddess of the West – another name for the Netherworld. She holds an *ankh*-sign in each hand, stretching one of them towards the king's nostrils.

In the middle of this scene we see the dead Pharaoh Tutankhamun. He is wearing a white headcloth and is facing the goddess in a receptive attitude, his arms hanging down. The text reads:

«*The good god, Neb-kheperu-re (Tutankhamun), bestowed with life eternally till infinity*».

Behind the Pharaoh, we see Anubis, the god with a canine head and human eyes. In one hand, he holds the symbol of life, while the other rests in a protective and guiding way over the shoulder of the king. It is a gesture of introduction, similar to the gesture of the *Ka* on the 3rd scene on the opposite north wall (see p. 83). He is described as

«*Anubis, at the head of the West, the great god who is in the place of embalming, Master of the Sky*».

On this part of the south wall, Tutankhamun is moving from left to right. This points to an internal relationship to the scene on the west wall. This scene has therefore to be seen together with what we see there: On the west wall, the barque of the Sungod passes through the night hours to resurrect in the morning.

Viewed in this light, we can understand this scene on the south wall as preparation of the *deceased Pharaoh to be ready to accompany the Sungod on his journey, which starts on the left of the west wall*. The sandals of the Pharaoh point to his still being in a realm between our world and the Beyond, in the same way as the 1st hour of the Amduat – which we find partly depicted on the west wall – is also still a realm in between the world of the living and the Beyond.

The continuation of the journey of Osiris-Tutankhamun to his resurrection as *Re-Osiris* in the east will later take place on the left part of the south wall (p. 95), as well as on the inside and the outside of the four gilded shrines that we will look at later (after page 96).

9. The west Wall

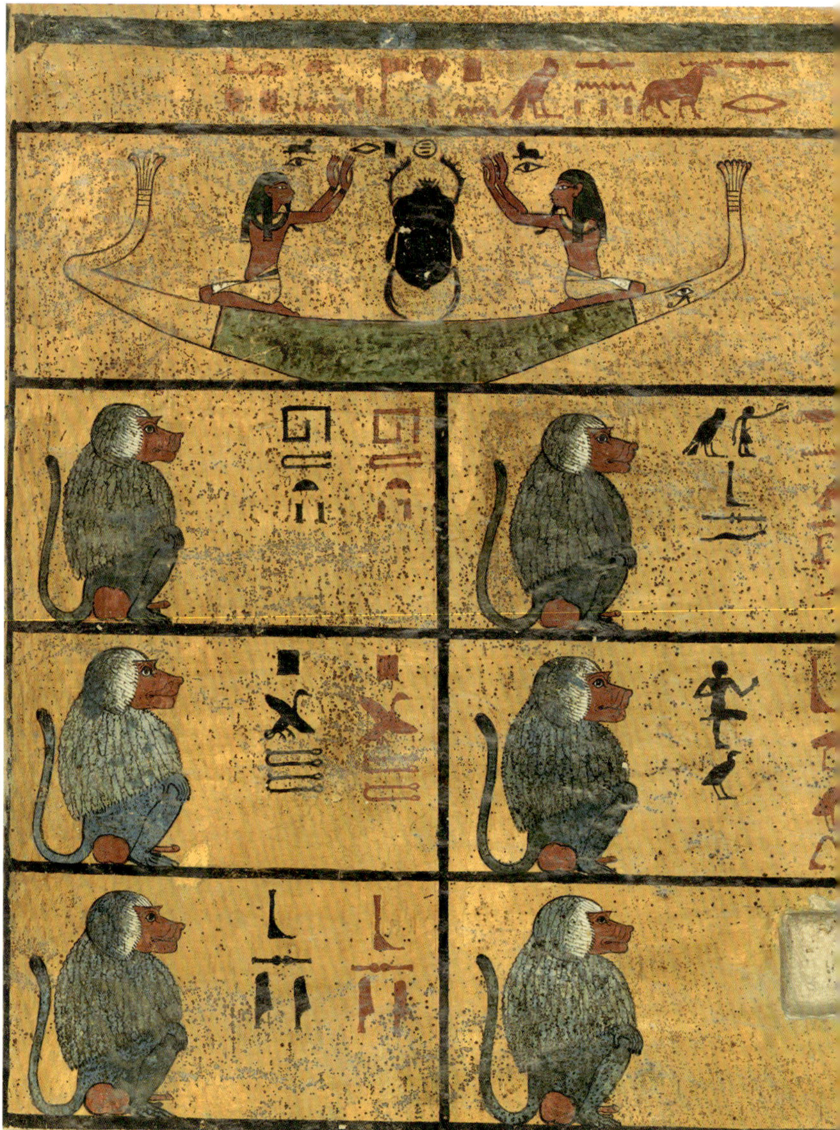

Fig. 69: The west wall.

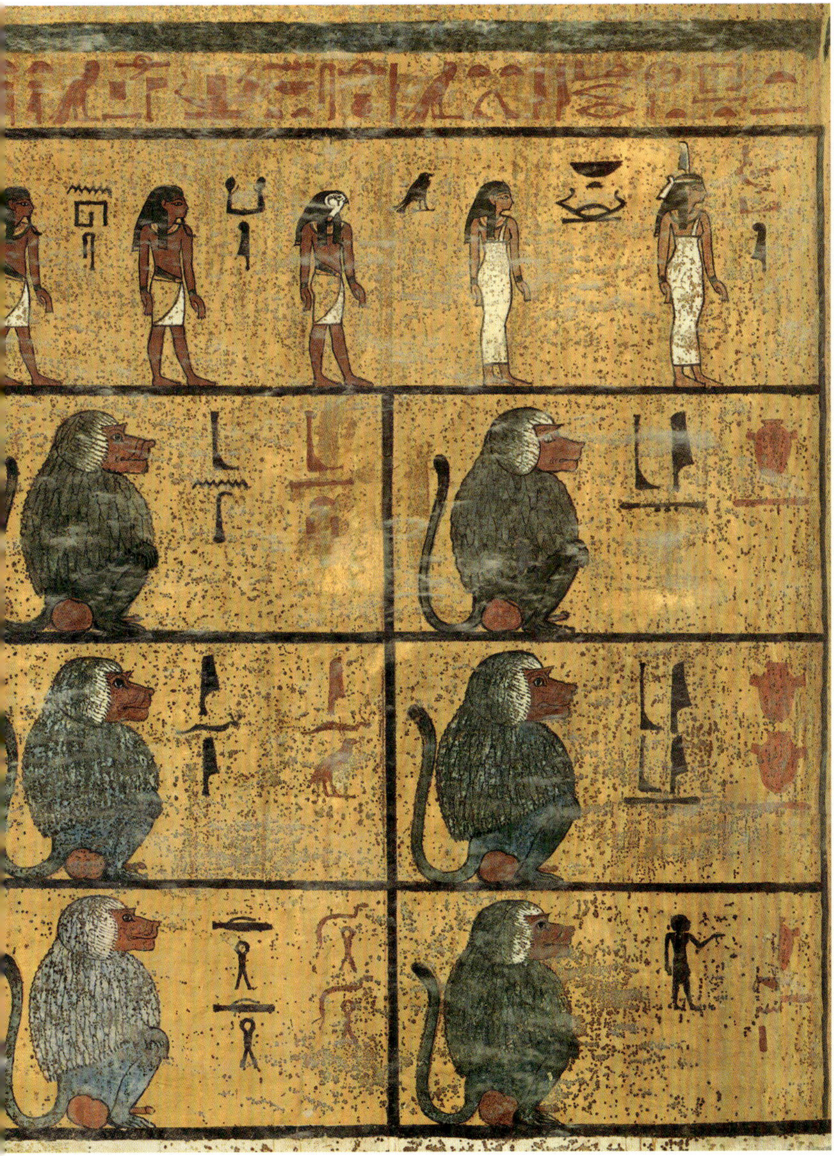

All along the top of the wall, we find again the hieroglyph 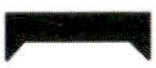 for heaven.

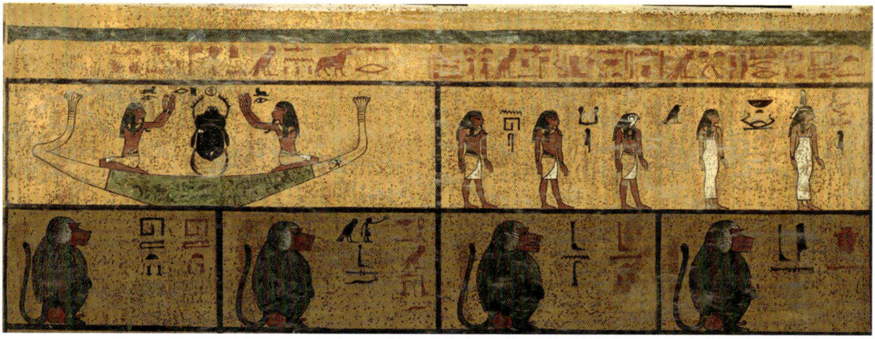

Fig. 70: The west wall, upper register.

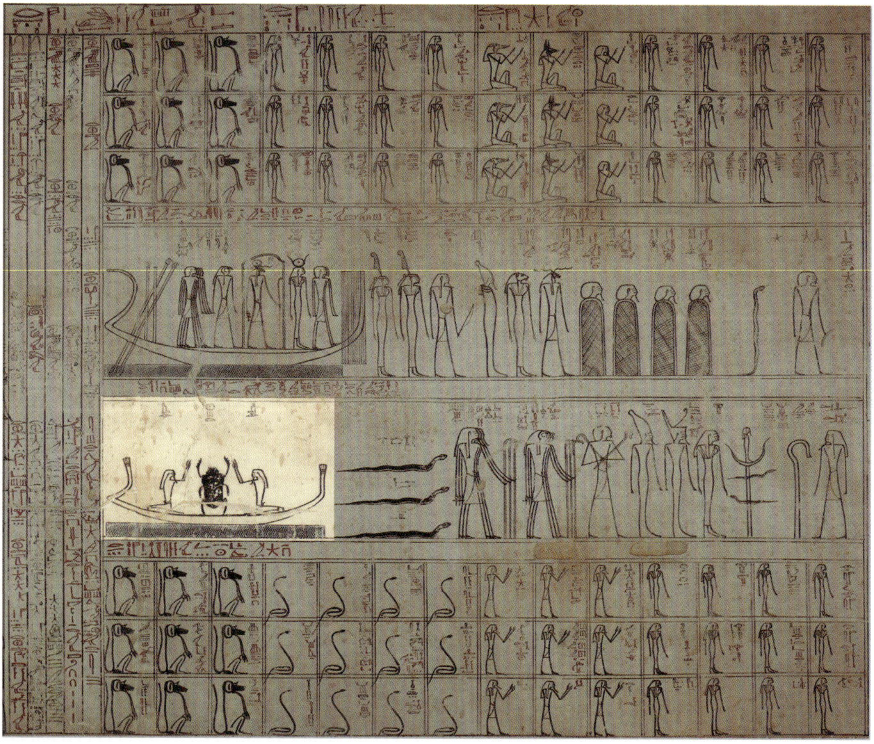

Fig. 71: The complete 1st hour of the *Amduat*.

9a. West Wall, upper Register

The west wall depicts scenes extracted from the 1st hour of the *Amduat* (see p. 23-25), the first complete Royal Book for the Afterlife, composed before the Amarna-period. As we have seen, the *Amduat* follows the circular movement of the sun. For the ancient Egyptians, the sun dies every day in the West at sunset, and rises again rejuvenated in the morning, overcoming its death by the night-journey. In the same way, the dead Pharaoh can, according to this ancient belief, overcome death, when the Pharaoh's *Ba*-soul is finally able to follow his father, the Sungod, on his journey through the dark night.

The upper register (fig. 70) shows a scarab in a barque. This scene is similar to the lower half of the middle register of the 1st hour of the *Amduat* (see fig. 71). In the barque, we see the scarab, symbol for the rejuvenated, resurrected Sungod. It is worshipped by two kneeling figures of *Osiris*, whose divine nature is represented by their hooked beards. Each figure is named *Osiris*; here the two represent Osiris-Tutankhamun.

To the right of the barque (fig. 70), we see five divinities: «*The goddess Ma'at*», «*the Mistress of the barque*», «*Horus*», «*Bull (master) of Ma'at*» (= the power of Ma'at) and «*Nehes*». Above this scene, we see a line of text in red hieroglyphs. It is from the *Amduat*: «*The two Ma'at-goddesses tow this god in the night barque, passing through the gateway of this region, [gateway] through which this god passes as a ram*».

The word *ram* in this text is one of the hieroglyphs for writing the word *Ba*-soul. It is in this form of the ram that the Sungod passes through the night-world in his barque. In the course of his night-journey *Re* unites with the Lord of the Netherworld *Osiris*. This fusion in the underworld has been summarised by the ancient Egyptians: «*Osiris, he is the Ba of Re, and Re is the Ba of Osiris*» (see fig. 92 on p. 109).

The night barque is for the Sungod's nocturnal journey in the Beyond. After his rebirth at dawn, he leaves it to embark on the day barque for his journey in the day-world. The barque is towed by *Ma'at* and her *Ka*, one of the examples of *the omnipresent duality in Egyptian thought*, other examples being the two lands of Upper and Lower Egypt and the red and the white crown.

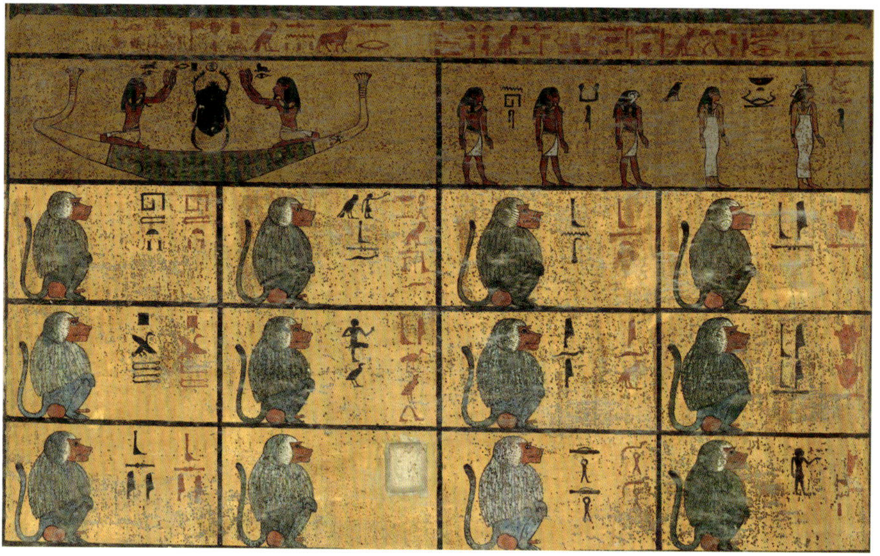

Fig. 72: The west wall, lower register.

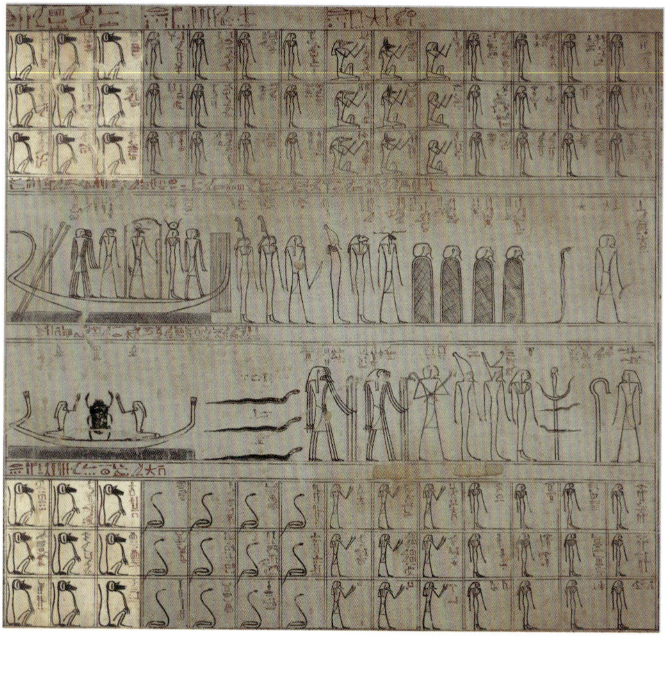

Fig. 73: 1st hour of the original *Amduat* with two times nine baboons.

9b. West Wall, lower Register

This lower part of the west wall is divided into twelve rectangles, each one including an identical baboon. These twelve baboons denote the twelve hours of the night journey of the Sungod (fig. 72). This is contrary to the original *Amduat*, where two times nine baboons, divided into the upper and the lower register, are welcoming the barque of the Sungod, exclaiming joy (see fig. 73).

Not only their number twelve, but also the role and function of these baboons seems different from the original *Amduat*. There the baboons welcome and acclaim the entry of the Sungod into the Netherworld, while here these animals point rather to their role of an *activated, continuous, directed energy flow throughout the twelve hours*. This interpretation is confirmed by the remarkable erect penis of all twelve baboons (fig. 74).

The names of these baboons are written in black, and to the right in red. The black text gives the name of the baboon in enigmatic writing, while the red colour is an explanation in normal hieroglyphs. The enigmatic writing points to something really important. The names of the baboons are for instance (1) *Heart of the earth*, (3) *Who praises with his fame*, (5) *Favourite of the earth*, (7) *Dancer*, (8) *Shrieker*, (12) *The flaming one*. In the Amduat, we read that these baboons «are opening (the gate) for the great *Ba*-soul», and that «they make music for Re when he enters the Netherworld».

It should be pointed out that in nature these baboons are related to the rising sun, which they greet in the morning with noisy screams. These baboons thus represent the *acclamation of these animals for the Sungod at the time of sunrise*.

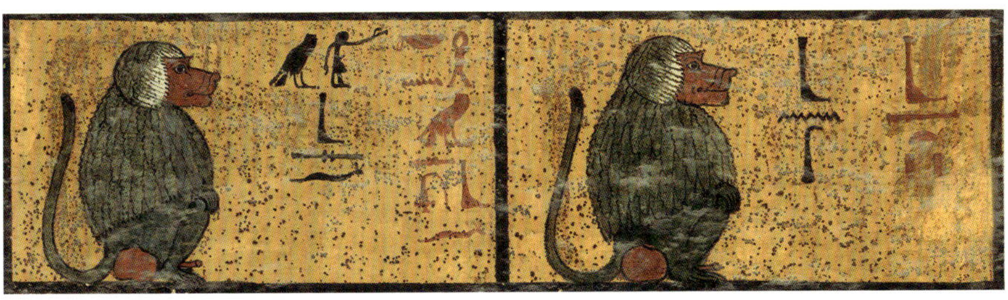

Fig. 74: Picture of two baboons enlarged.

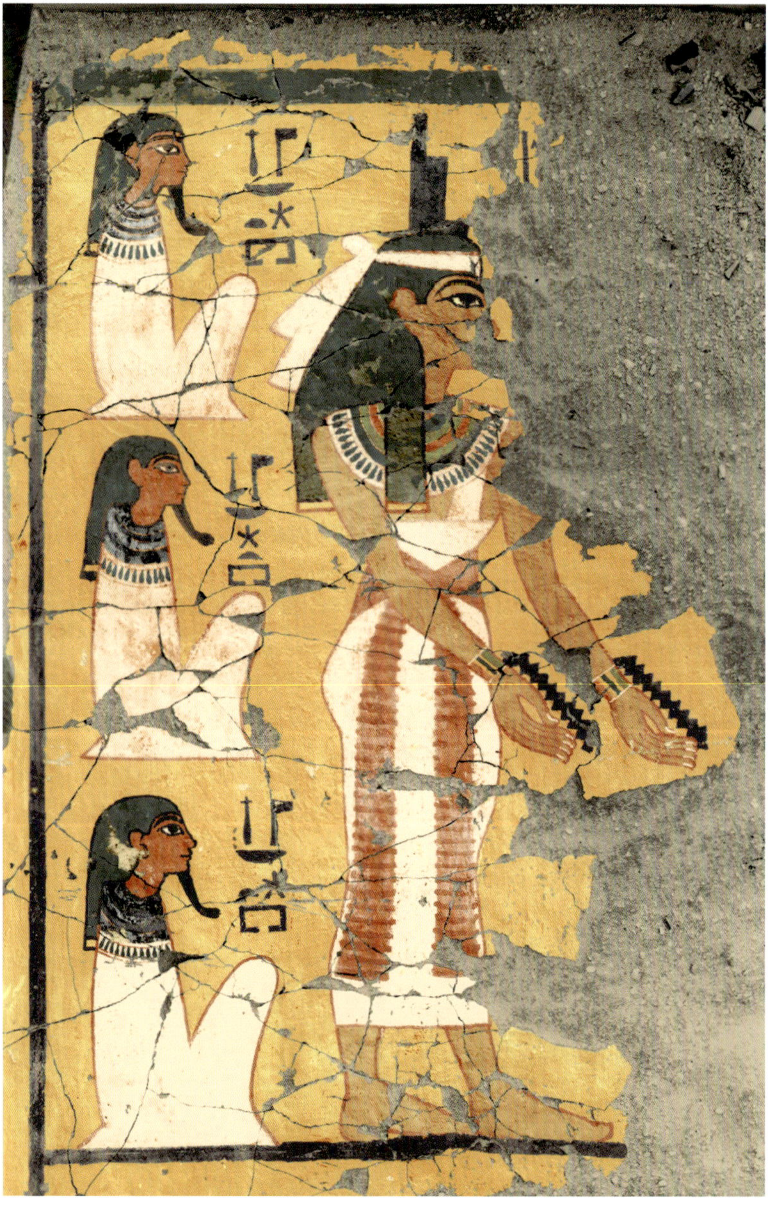

Fig. 75: Reconstructed detail of south wall, left part.

10. South Wall, left Part – the Completion of the solar Circle

Howard Carter was forced to destroy this part of the South wall when the gilded shrines were being brought out of the burial chamber. The goddess Isis and three other squatting gods can thus no longer be seen.

However, Carter secured the fragments that were to be kept in a storeroom of the Service of Antiquities. *Factum Arte* created in painstaking work a colour facsimile of these fragments, based on black and white photos taken at the time.

Here, in fig. 75, we see the goddess Isis with the hieroglyph of a throne on her head. Isis, like Nut, whom we saw in the middle of the North wall, is making the same welcoming *nini* gesture. The text that belongs to Isis is preserved on the wall: «*Mistress of the Sky, who offers welcome to the one whom she brought into the world. May she give life and health [...] to your nostrils eternally*». Isis, Hathor of the West and the goddess Nut are all dressed in a similar way, and are all named *Mistress of the Sky*. According to the myth, it is Isis who gave birth to Horus, the son of her murdered husband Osiris. Horus then became the first Pharaoh, and ever since all Pharaohs are Horus, sons of Isis.

This scene links up with the corner of the east wall, the beginning of the funeral procession. We can understand this scene with the welcome gesture of mother Isis to her son Tutankhamun, as pointing to the king's new birth, to his resurrection as *Re-Osiris*, similar to the rising sun on the morning horizon.

Thus this scene *completes the circle of death and resurrection*, as Isis was the first goddess that we saw at the feet of the mummy on the east wall. This scene on the south wall is also complementary to the 2nd scene on the north wall. There the female divinity Nut welcomes and blesses the dead Pharaoh with her divine water and leads him to Osiris to become Osiris-Tutankhamun. Here Isis welcomes the king to his resurrection as Re-Osiris.

The three superimposed gods squatting behind Isis complete the decoration on the left side of the south wall. They are all identified as «*Great god, Lord of the Duat*». This is not a reference to their actual identity, nature or function. They symbolise in general the many divinities which populate the Netherworld. In Ancient Egypt, the number three indicates their plurality.

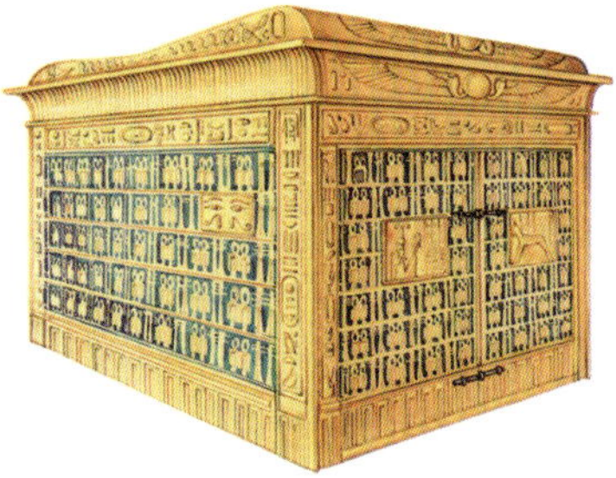

Shrine I

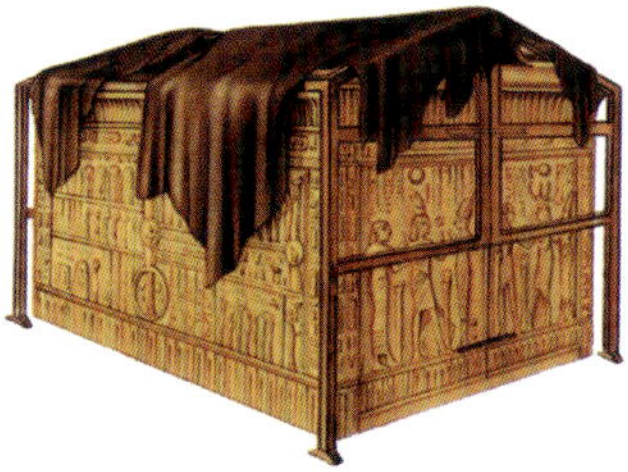

Linen pall on a wooden stand with Shrine II.

Shrine II

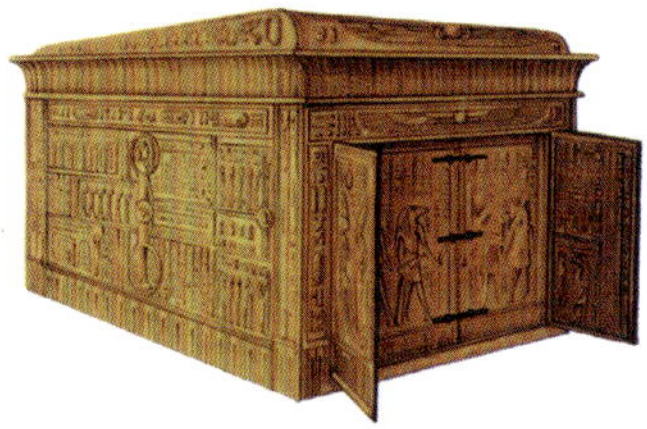

Shrine III

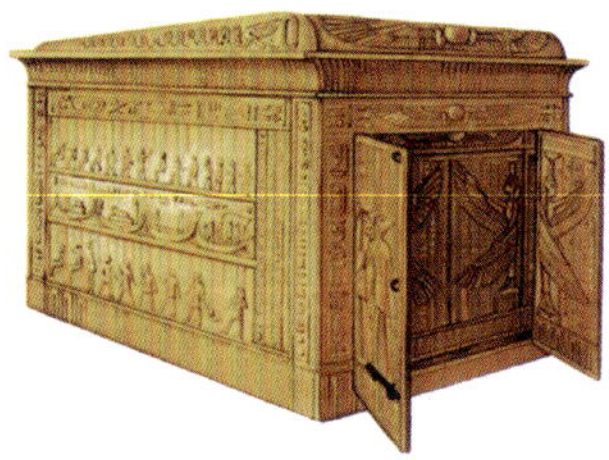

Shrine IV

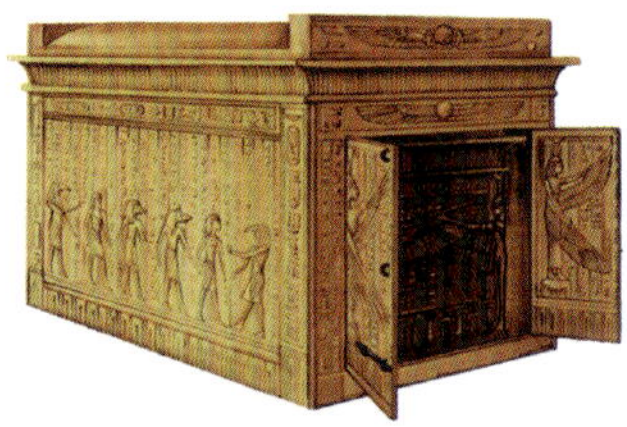

Sarcophagus

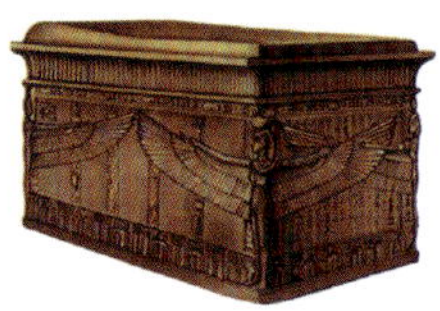

Fig. 76: The shrines I-IV around the quartzite sarcophagus.

11. The four Shrines around the quartzite Sarcophagus

The four shrines around the sarcophagus are made of 3 cm thick imported cedar wood. Both their inner and outer surfaces are covered with thin leaves of gold foil, on which religious representations and inscriptions can be found (fig. 76).

To these four shrines, Howard Carter gave the numbers I to IV, following the sequence as they appeared to the discoverer. However, for our purpose here, *this order must be reversed.* Thus the shrines will be presented in the sequence in which the ancient Egyptians intended and understood them. Following their order, we start with the inside decoration of the smallest Shrine IV, and end our reflection with the outside of the largest Shrine I.

What we know about the text and representations of the four shrines is due above all to the painstaking work of the Russian-French Egyptologist Alexandre Piankoff (1897-1966). During World War II, he worked on the recording of these shrines, as well as on the translation of their texts and published his findings in 1952, as we shall now see in detail.

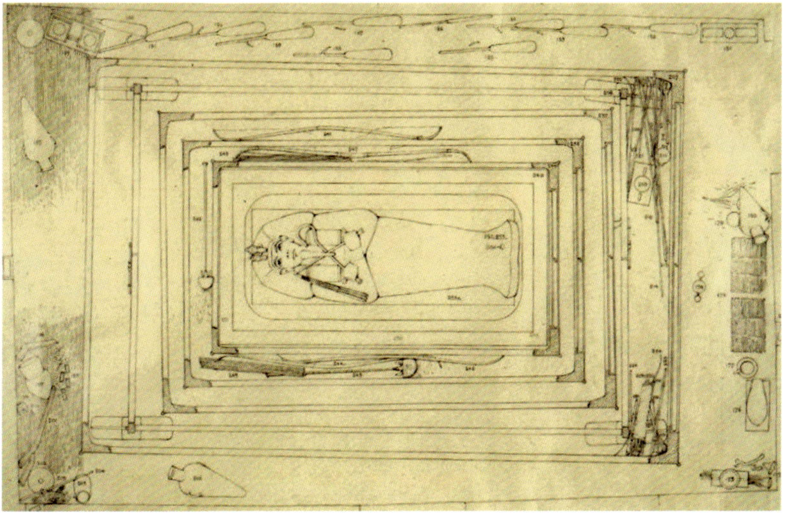

Fig. 77: Drawing by H. Carter of the sarcophagus, surrounded by the four gilded shrines.

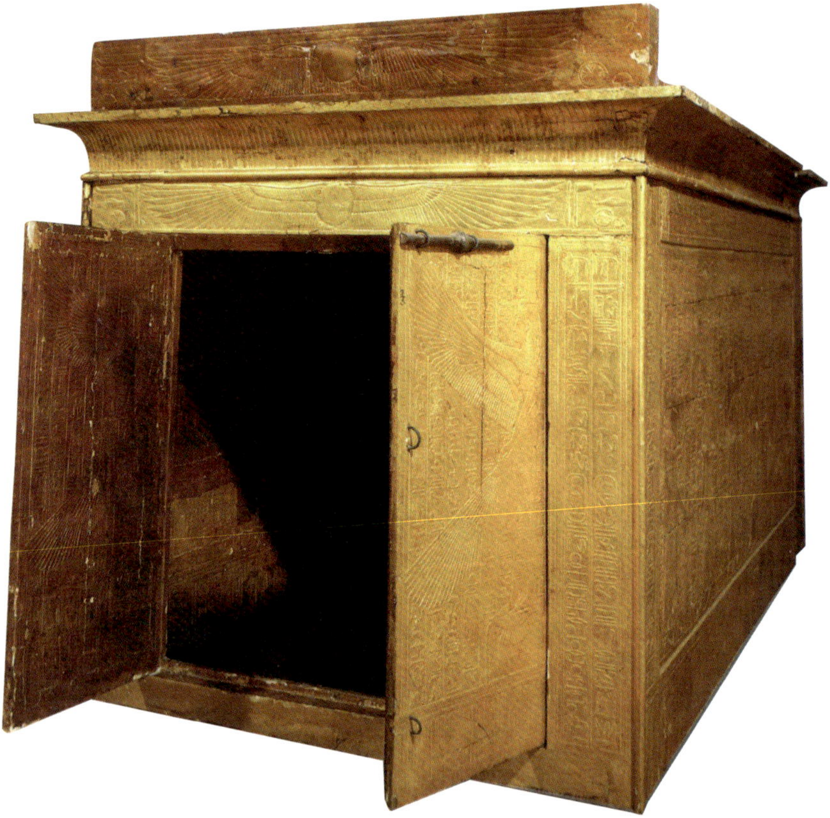

Fig. 78: The gilded Shrine IV.

12a. The smallest Shrine IV, exterior

The entire Shrine IV features protecting divinities on the outside that help Osiris-Tutankhamun to ward off his enemies (fig. 78).

The outside and the inside of the door-leaves of Shrine IV as well as its back side show representations of the goddesses *Isis* and her sister *Nephthys* (fig. 79). With their winged arms, they protect and accompany the dead king Osiris-Tutankhamun, thus assuring his resurrection.

We will now follow the journey of Osiris-Tutankhamun up to his transformation into *Re-Osiris*.

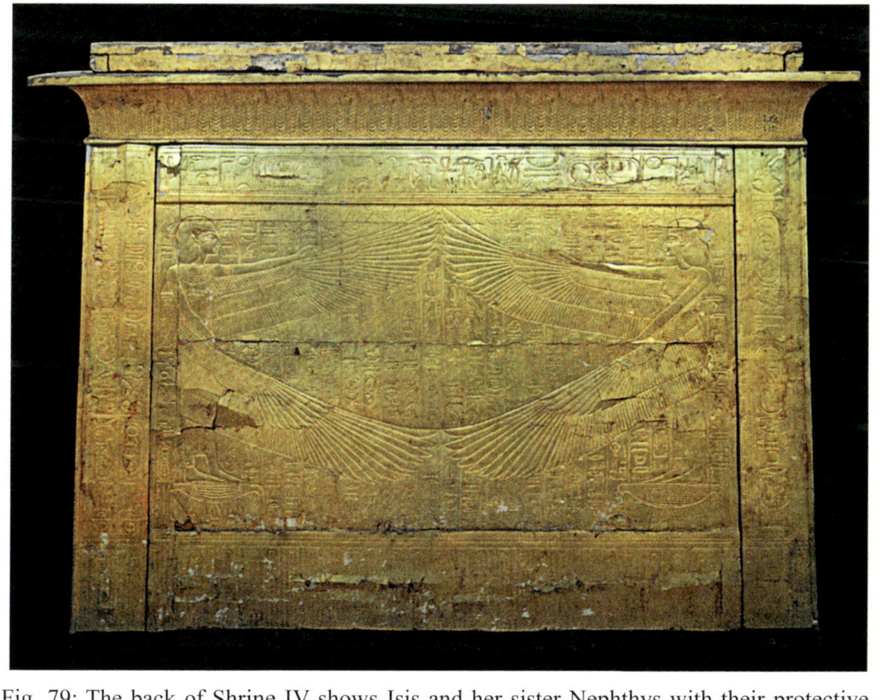

Fig. 79: The back of Shrine IV shows Isis and her sister Nephthys with their protective winged arms.

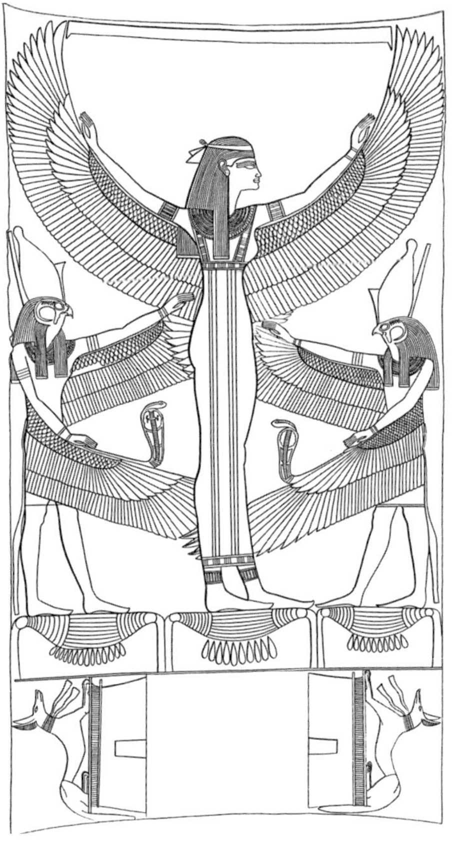

Fig. 80: The picture of the goddess Nut on the ceiling of Shrine IV.

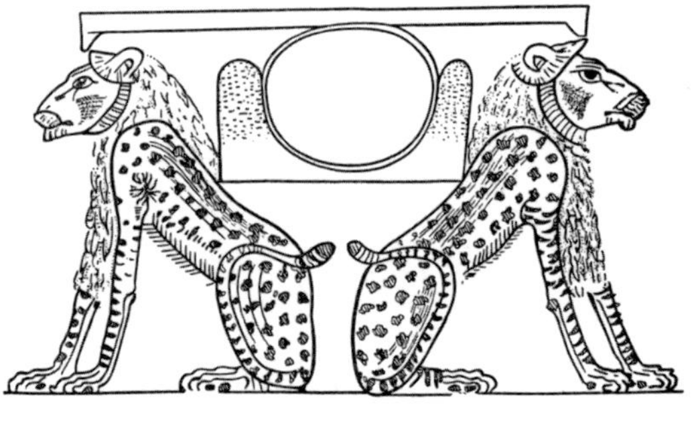

Fig. 81: Image inside Shrine IV: *The Lions of Yesterday and Tomorrow.* Between them the sun-disc above the sign for the horizon, symbol for the ceaseless course of the sun.

12b. Shrine IV, interior

On the interior ceiling of Shrine IV, the sky goddess *Nut* spreads her protecting wings over the sarcophagus of the king (fig. 80). We have already seen the goddess *Nut* on the north wall of the burial chamber (p. 74-75). There, by making the *nini*-gesture, she welcomes the deceased king «*as the one she has given birth to*». On this ceiling, above the head of *Nut*, is written: «*Words spoken by Osiris-Tutankhamun: Mother Nut, spread your wings over me, encircle me with your arms in health and in life that I may be inside you, that you may be my protection! I am your son, Osiris-Tutankhamun* ...»

Below the wings we can read: «*I shall be your protection, that your limbs be complete, like Re, while you will live forever and everlastingly.*» This text shows that Nut, the feminine goddess of heaven, will complete again the dissolved limbs of the deceased body of Osiris-Tutankhamun. These words point to an approach of the deceased, restored king Osiris-Tutankhamun to his father, the Sungod Re, as the goal of the forthcoming process of their reunion, as we shall see.

The interor sidewalls of Shrine IV represent in text and images the *beginning of creation*. This also symbolises the beginning of the restoration of the deceased and dismembered Osiris-Tutankhamun for his reunification and thus resurrection with his father, the Sungod *Re*, as *Re-Osiris*.

The text on the interior back wall and on the inner two side panels is a monologue by the Sungod Re as creator of the world (Chapter 17 of the *Book of the Dead*). It describes how Re, by his own creative effort, first emerged out of the primeval waters *Nun*, creating heaven and earth. This myth recalls the origin of the creation of the light of the sun.

This first text can be understood as knowledge in support of the resurrection of the king Tutankhamun, who, after his death, also dissolved as Osiris in the primeval waters *Nun*. In order to resurrect from this state, the king will now have to join and then follow his father, the Sungod Re, who knows the secret of self-creation and thus of eternal self-rejuvenation. By being able to join the Sungod – the role-model for eternal rejuvenation for the ancient Egyptians – the king will be able to emerge out of the primeval waters of *Nun* again, and thus be able to follow the never-ending course of the sun (fig. 81).

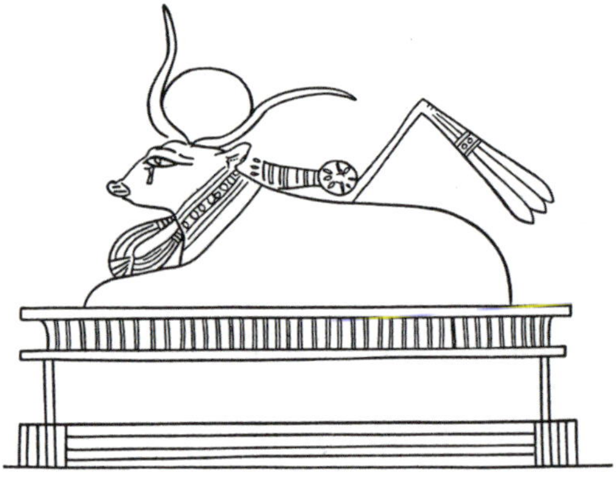

Fig. 82: Diagram of the image of the divine cow from the interior of Shrine IV.

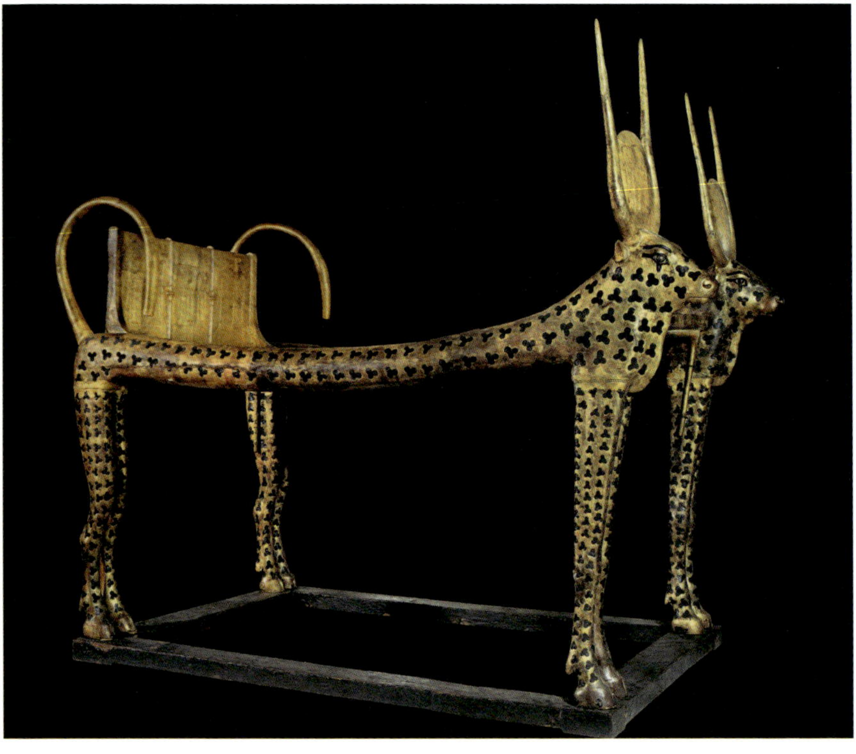

Fig. 83: The cow-bier, representing the cosmic *Mehet-weret*, found in the tomb of Tutankhamun.

12b. Shrine IV, interior

Of the many representations given on the interior walls of Shrine IV, we shall now just look at two other pictures that follow the one that we saw in figure 81.

First we shall contemplate the image of the divine celestial cow *Mehet-weret* (fig. 82). Her name means «the Great Flood». However, given her activity as female consort of *Nun*, the primeval water, her name is more accurately translated as *The Great Swimmer*. As a personification of primeval matter she is the one, who – according to the creation myth – at the beginning of creation collected and paradoxically carried the self-creating Sungod out of the primeval water *Nun* on her back or between her horns (fig. 84). This celestial cow is here the one who will also bring Osiris-Tutankhamun back to life, enabling him to join his father Re and become *Osiris-Re*.

The aim of this process will later (inside the largest Shrine I) be represented in The *Book of the Heavenly Cow*. This will round off our knowledge of the mysterious regenerative power of this divine female mother-animal.

The text here at the beginning of the process (Chapter 17 of the B*ook of the Dead*) and the text inside the largest Shrine I, named *The Book of the Heavenly Cow* (p. 119), together represent the first and the final stages of the king's transformation: the birth of the Sungod out of the primeval water Nun, and his elevation into heaven as resurrected *Osiris-Re* on the back of the divine cow.

One of the three biers found in the antechamber of the tomb of Tutankhamun also shows a representation of the divine cow (fig. 83). Inside its cosmic body – represented by the stars – this cow-bier carries the mummy of the deceased king through the darkness of the night to his resurrection in the morning (fig. 84).

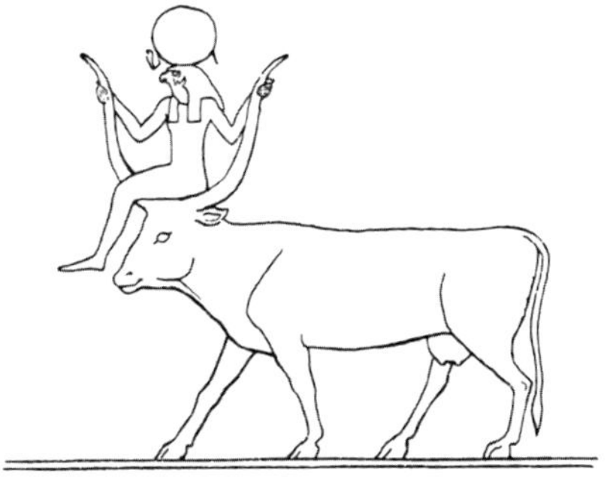

Fig. 84: The Sungod riding between the horns of the divine cow.

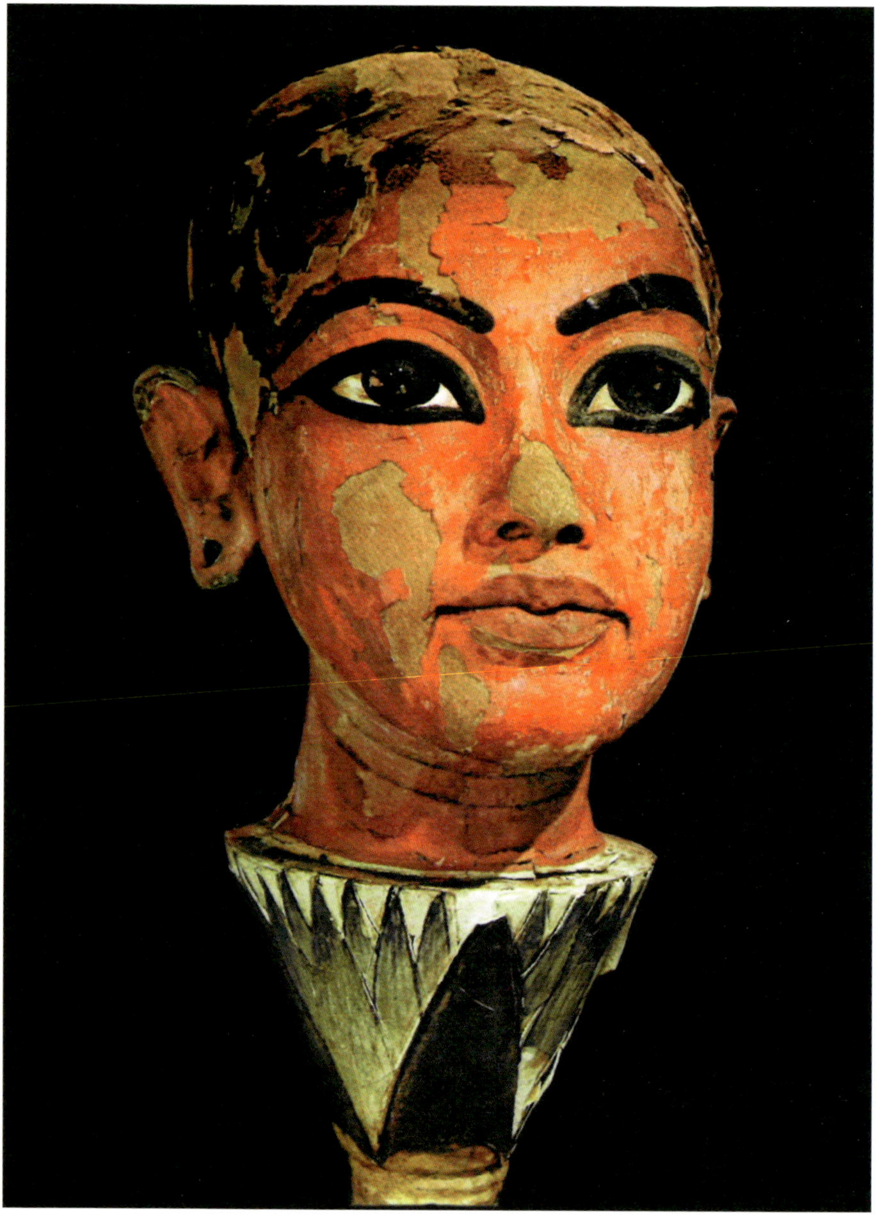

Fig. 85: Renewed and resurrected Tutankhamun as Sungod, rising from a lotus-flower.

12b. Shrine IV, interior

A further image inside Shrine IV will conclude our reflections on the resurrection of Tutankhamun. It is the lotus-flower, which in Ancient Egypt was also a common symbol for regeneration, almost of the same importance as the scarab. We have an image of this lotus-flower at the end of the text inside Shrine IV (fig. 86).

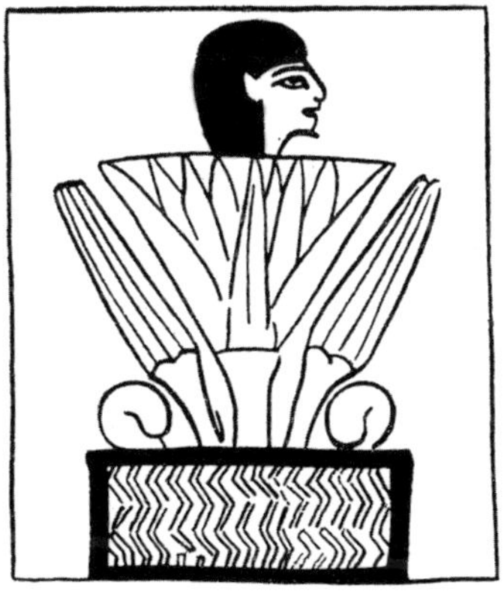

Fig. 86: Nefertem, the son of Sekhmet emerges out of a lotus-flower.

One of the most moving sculptures of Tutankhamun, found in his tomb, shows the head of the resurrected king Tutankhamun as a new, young Sungod, emerging from the lotus-flower (fig. 85). According to the myth, the god *Nefertem*, the son of the lion-goddess *Sekhmet*, emerged from the lotus-flower. This god *Nefertem* – another symbol for the renewed Sungod – is identified here with the resurrected Tutankhamun.

In the same way as the lotus-flower has to grow through and out of muddy water, the deceased Tutankhamun – according to the text that accompanies figure 86 – has to pass through the many dangers of the Netherworld. This process of his rejuvenation will continue on Shrine III.

The text that goes with this representation says that the Sungod Re «*is in his egg, shining in his disk that appears on his horizon*». The motif of the Sungod who shines "in his egg that is his disk" points to the mysterious self-creation of the Sungod. Out of the seemingly lifeless egg that consists, seen symbolically, just of four elements – namely the shell, the egg-white, the skin around it and the yellow yolk – *life can emerge*. This happens by simple hatching, in the same way as the Sungod came out by himself from the primeval waters of *Nun*, carried by the celestial cow.

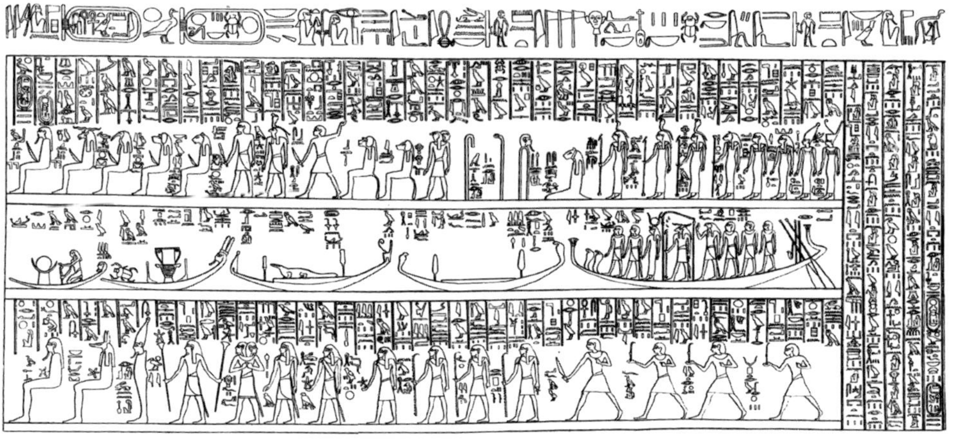

Fig. 87: The second hour of the *Amduat* as seen on Shrine III.

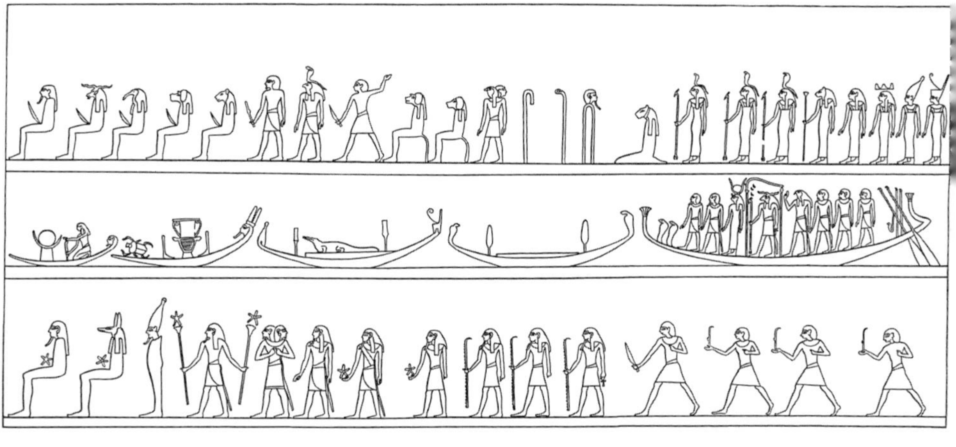

Fig. 88: Schema of the second hour of the *Amduat*.

13a. Shrine III, exterior, left Side

On the two outer side-panels of the larger Shrine III, we see two incomplete representations of two hours of the *Amduat*. We have already seen parts of the first hour of this book painted on the west wall of the burial chamber (on p. 90 and 92).

Looking at the outside of the shrine from its door, we see on the left side the *second hour of the Amduat* (fig. 87 and 88). It is presented as fertile land, watered by the primeval ocean *Nun*. In the middle part or register, we see the barque of the Sungod, accompanied by four other boats, «*which are in the earth*», carrying provisions and symbolic signs. In this hour the process of transformation in the Beyond starts to flow; the water in the depth of the earth carries the ships along.

This hour represents the beginning of the flow of the process to the rejuvenation of the deceased king Osiris-Tutankhamun. He will have to follow his father, the Sungod Re, on his barque to complete the journey through the night. Thus, in the morning, he can finally reunite with him and will rise as the new sun *Re-Osiris*.

The *Amduat* shows a clearly ordered structure of the hours of the night in three horizontal parts or registers.

This gives a helpful orientation for the journey of the Sungod through the night. This dark night world, which today we call the *unconscious*, has a reliable structure of its own. For modern depth psychology it is a well-known fact that the unconscious world also contains an ordering force that can regulate and structure human transformation and development. Yet this order *has to be known and respected* by those who enter this other world, as the *Amduat* repeatedly emphasises.

The direction of the movement of the second hour of the *Amduat*, as well as that of the sixth hour of the *Amduat*, which we shall look at on the next page, flows away from the door of the shrine to the back of the shrine.

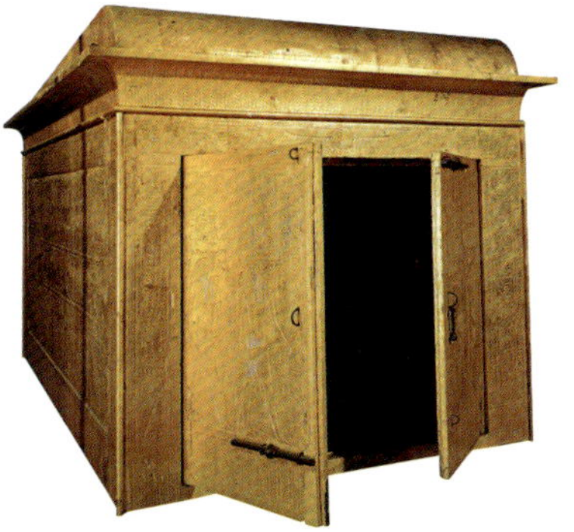

Fig. 89: Shrine III.

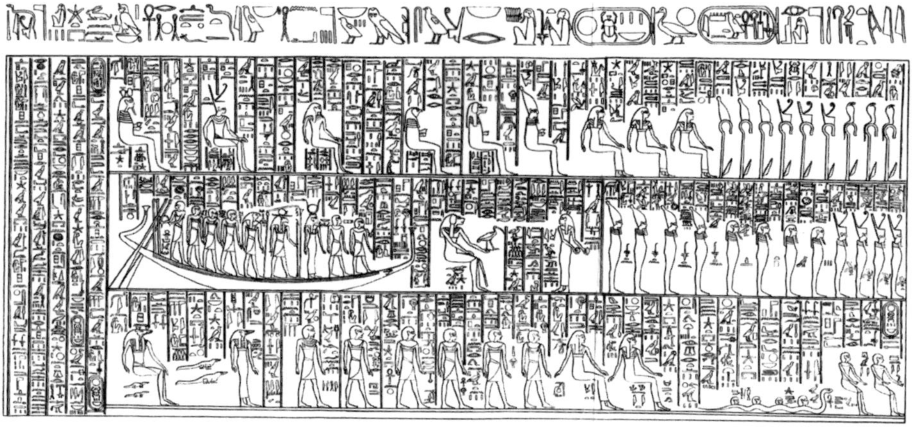

Fig. 90: The sixth hour of the Amduat as seen on Shrine III.

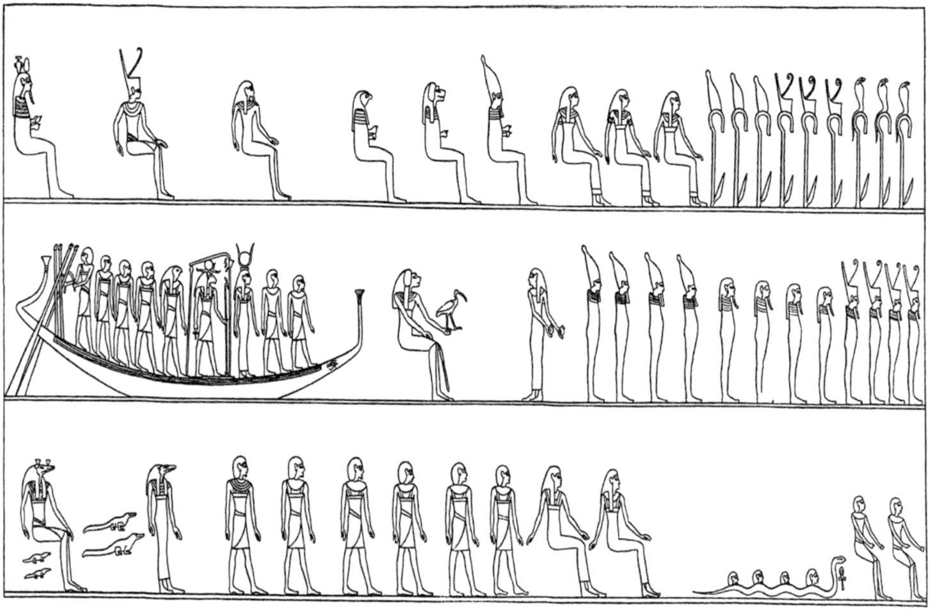

Fig. 91: Schema of the sixth hour of the Amduat as seen on Shrine III.

13b. Shrine III, exterior, right Side

In the *sixth hour of the Amduat* (fig. 90 and 91) we enter the *«waterhole of those of the Netherworld»*, filled again with the primeval water *Nun* and its regenerative power. In these uttermost depths, the first unification of the light of the night-sun Re as *Ba*-soul and the *Ba*-soul of the corpse of Osiris-Tutankhamun takes place, and thus, in the depth of the night, the light of the sun is rekindled. This hour is called the *«Arrival pointing to the right way»*.

The nascent new life is heralded by the semi-raised position of beings in the upper and lower register. Here, where the Ba-soul of the Sungod joins the Ba-soul of the body of the deceased king Osiris-Tutankhamun (fig. 92), here in the deepest *Nun, The Great Swimmer* will find, reassemble and carry up the renewed Sungod. Here too, as before in the 2nd hour, the direction of the movement of the 6th hour flows away from the door of the shrine. This process will continue on the second-largest shrine, on Shrine II.

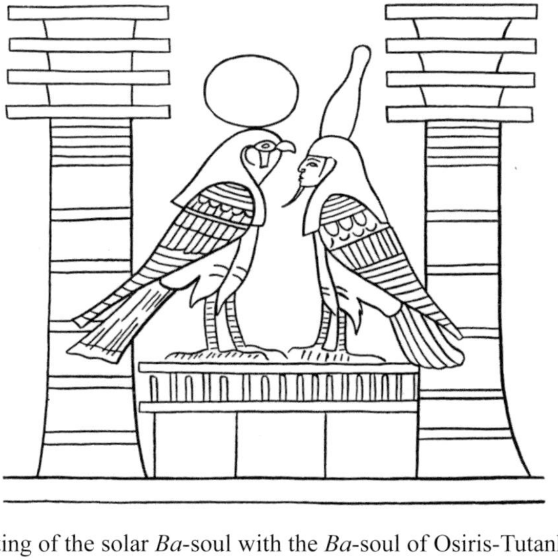

Fig. 92: The meeting of the solar *Ba*-soul with the *Ba*-soul of Osiris-Tutankhamun, joining in a two-oneness in the depth of the night, represented inside Shrine IV.

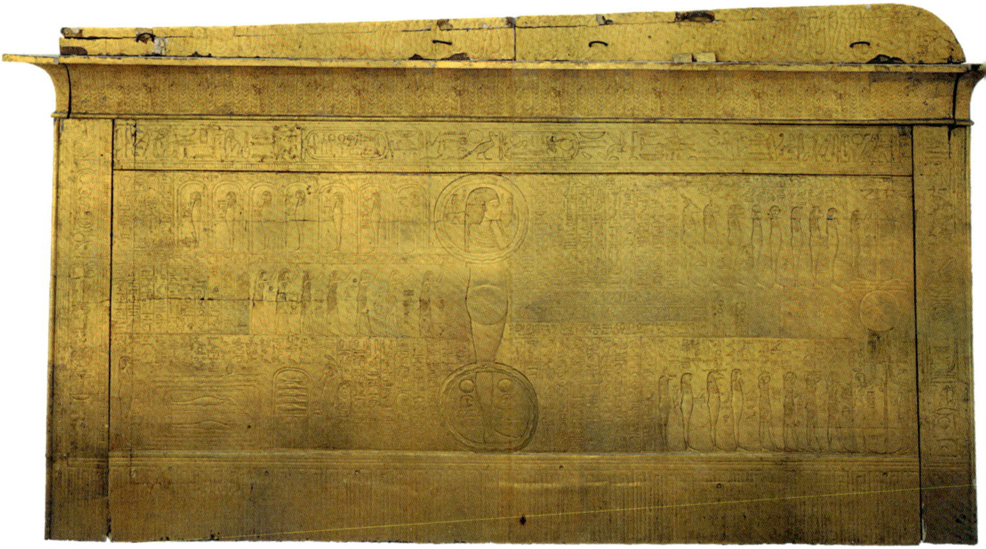

Fig. 93: Part A of the enigmatic *Book for the Afterlife* on Shrine II.

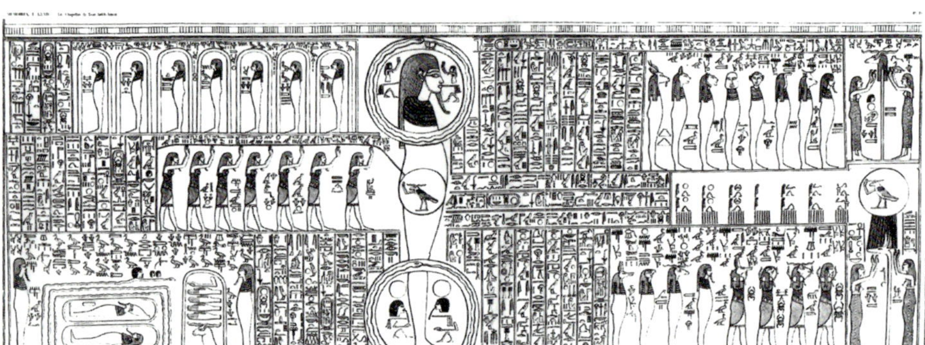

Fig. 94a: Schema of part A of the enigmatic *Book for the Afterlife* on Shrine II.

14a. Shrine II, exterior, Part A

Similar to the two hours of the *Amduat* on the outside of Shrine III, we also find on the outside panels of Shrine II two parts of a *Book for the Afterlife* that from what we know today, has no parallels. Most of the text on this Shrine II is not in common hieroglyphic writing, but in cryptography. In Ancient Egypt, this writing usually pointed to something very important or special.

In order to become familiar with these two panels, we follow the interpretation of Erik Hornung, who suggested looking first at the left side of the shrine (Part A, fig. 93/94) and then moving to its right side (Part B). This sequence is similar to Shrine III, where the second hour was also represented on the left side, while the second part, the sixth hour, was given on the right side.

Part A speaks of the darkness and the place of destruction, while Part B is characterised by the light of the many suns and stars. In the middle of Part A, we see a large image of a mummified divine figure, extending over all three registers. Around the head and around the feet of this figure, there is a huge serpent that has its tail in its mouth, thus forming a circle. This is the first known representation of a so-called *Ouroboros*, symbol for a solid container for the infinite of the Beyond. Later on, this symbol of the *Ouroboros* became the central symbol of alchemy.

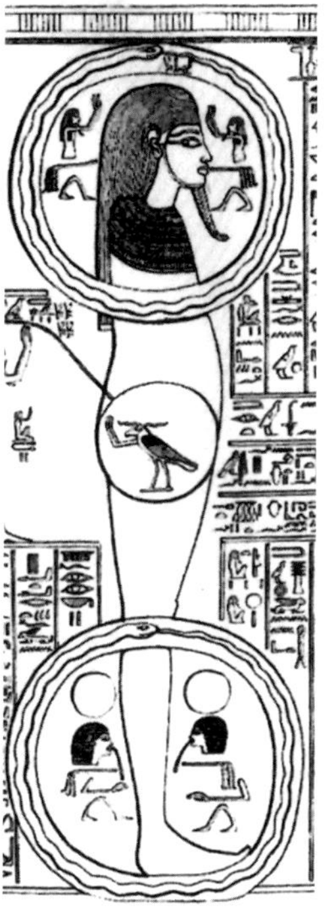

Fig. 94b: Detail of fig. 94a.

The text related to the divine figure (fig. 94b) speaks about the creation and destruction of time. John Darnell sees in this figure an emerging union of Re and Osiris.

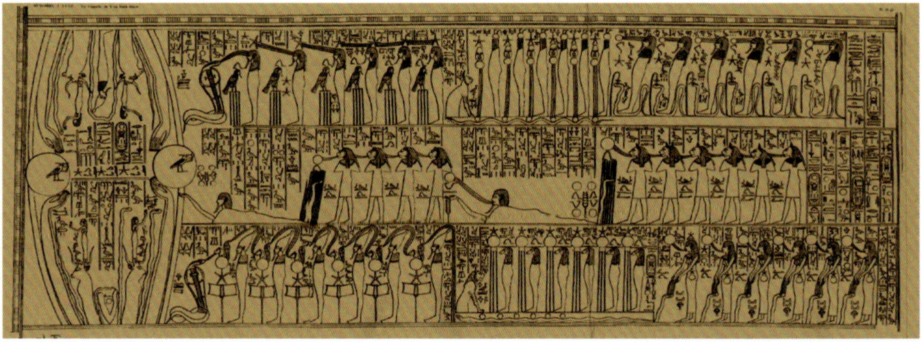

Fig. 95a: Gilded schema of Part B of the enigmatic *Book for the Afterlife* on Shrine II.

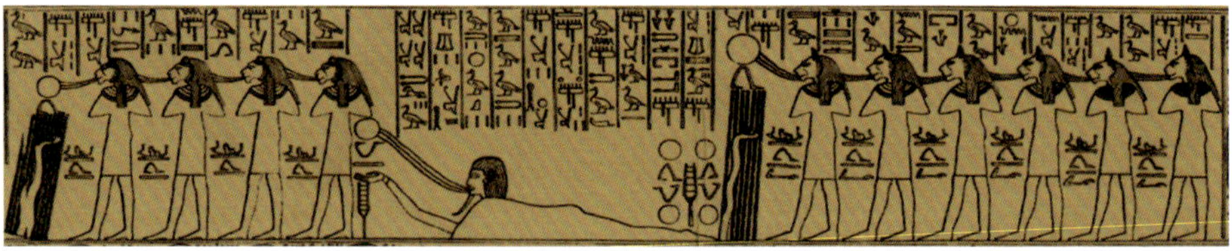

Fig. 95b: Detail of the Middle Register of fig. 95a.

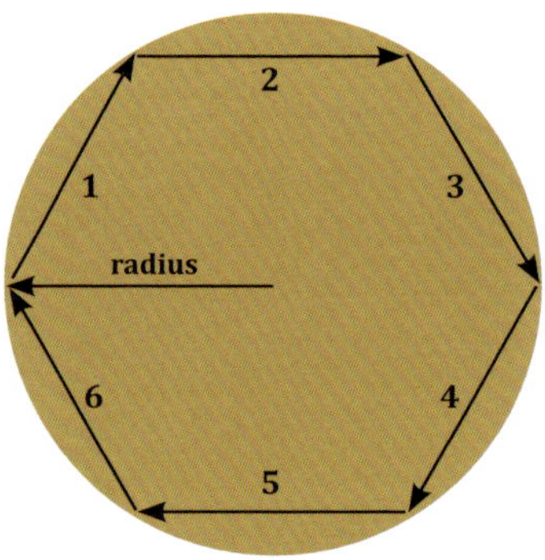

Fig. 96: Geometrically the six is connected to the perfect form, since a circle can be divided by its radius into six parts. The circle is the perfect form and as such, is a well-known symbol for totality and the godhead. Thus the hexagon is structured by the length of the radius, by god's measure, so to speak. Therefore, the number six is related to the whole of creation, the macrocosm and its creator.
In its dynamic aspect the circle is a cycle, which thus is also conntected to the number six.

14b. Shrine II, exterior, Part B

Part B of the second shrine has as its main feature many representations of the sun-disc. *All the anthropomorphic figures or mummies are looking toward the final scene at the end of the panel on its left side*. The mummies are met by different animals: serpents, a cat or a lion. The attention or energy-flow culminates in the end-scene, where we see a *representation of the whole cycle of the Sungod* with two sun-discs each containing a *Ba*-soul bird, held by four arms. Two are coming from the depth of the primeval water and two from the sky above. This could be understood as the further emerging of an awareness of the two-oneness that this process is leading to, the union of the mortal-immortal body with the light of the immortal Re.

The bodies of the figures or mummies of this Part B are illuminated by the rays or the voice of the Sungod Re and the *Ba*-souls of these figures. Text and picture repeatedly show that the light of a sun-disc or of a star is entering into the bodies of the figures or mummies. *This shows the gradual unification of the solar or cosmic (stars!) light of the Sungod Re with the bodily aspects of Osiris-Tutankhamun.*

In contrast to Part A, where we sometimes saw groups of seven or eight beings, in Part B, in the upper and the lower register, *we mainly find groups of six figures*. Six, being the perfect and complete division of a circle by its own radius, is accordingly the number of *perfect support of circular renewal* (see fig. 96). The dominance of the number six in the different groups could also be seen to relate to the sixth hour of the *Amduat*, which we found represented on Shrine III, on the same side of the outer panel (see p. 108-109).

In the middle register, we find 6 and 4 lion-headed creatures with hidden arms (see fig. 95b). This motif of the hidden arms is known from the sixth hour of *The Book of Gates*, where mummies carry the hidden corpse of the Sungod. Here, the lion-headed creatures seem to have a similar function. As the lion is a well-known symbol for rejuvenation and resurrection, we can – together with Alexandre Piankoff – understand this Part B as «*the refilling of the sun-disc*» for the renewed, rejuvenated Osiris-Tutankhamun, rising in the morning as Re-Osiris.

This process will continue on the largest shrine, on Shrine I.

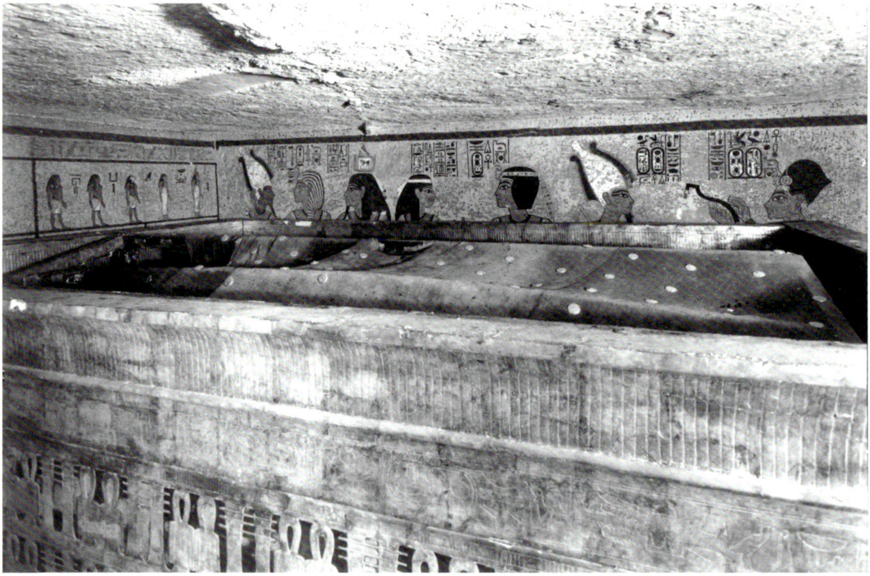

Fig. 97: Pall at the time of its discovery, lying on the stand of the shrine.

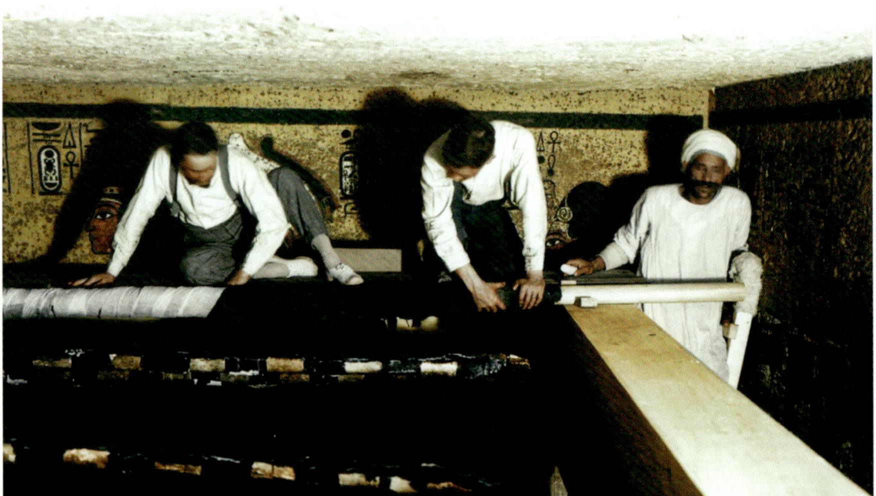

Fig. 98: Most careful winding-up of the pall by Howard Carter and his team. The wooden stand around Shrine II is partly visible in the lower left part of the picture. Coloured by Griffith Institute, University of Oxford.

15. The Pall

A wooden structure with a coarsely woven linen pall was found between Shrine II and Shrine I (see fig. 76). This fabric was decorated with large marguerites (daisy-like flowers) of gilded bronze. A man in Carter's team described the fabric as «like a night sky spangled with stars» (see fig. 99).

This woven linen pall could be interpreted as a symbol for a subtle night-sky-container for the restored individual soul of the deceased king, ready for resurrection, as we will now see in detail in Shrine I.

Unfortunately, the fabric was ruined when it was left out in the open, during a period when Carter's American team was prevented from working in the tomb and laboratory.

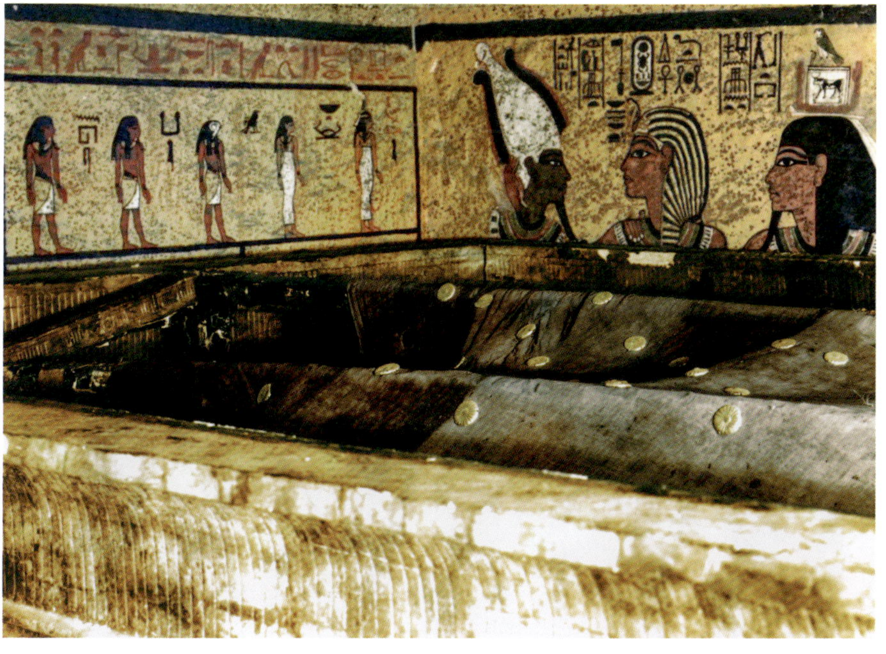

Fig. 99: Coloured close-up view of the pall: the marguerite flowers on the pall.

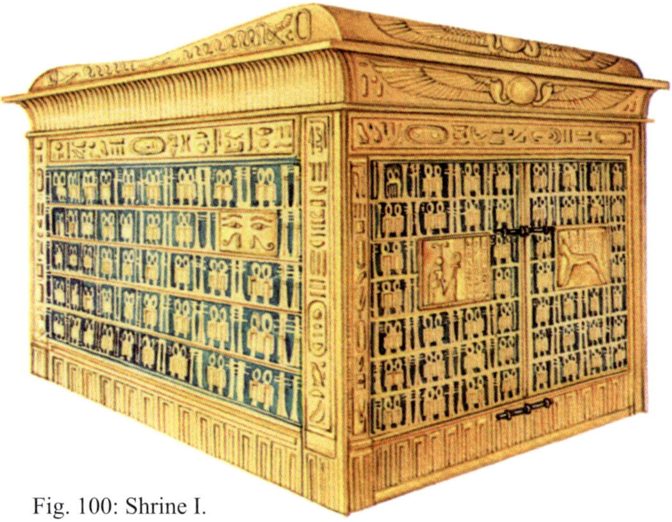

Fig. 100: Shrine I.

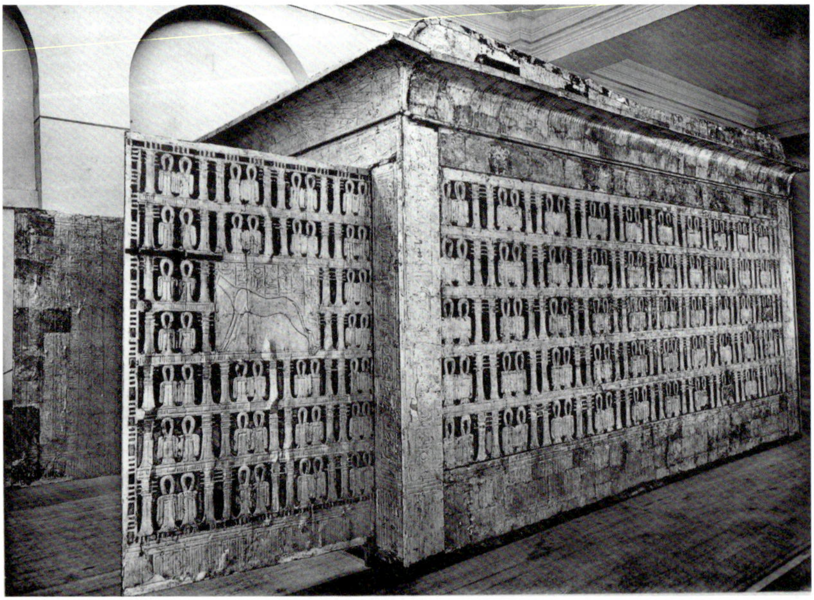

Fig. 101: Shrine I before it was placed under a glass-cover for protection.
Egyptian Museum, Cairo.

16a. Shrine I, outside

The forms of all four shrines are symbolic. While the smallest shrine resembles the form of a pre-dynastic temple of northern Egypt, the second and the third shrine were models of the pre-dynastic temples of the South. This Shrine I (fig. 100), the largest and outermost one, resembles the pavilion in which the king renewed his power and energy during the so-called *Sed*-festival, the royal jubilee (see glossary).

The external panels of the Shrine I are inlaid with blue faïence and bear alternate pairs of *djet*-pillars, symbol of Osiris and pairs of *tit*-knots, associated with Isis. The *tit* was often called the "knot of Isis" or the "blood of Isis", as amulets of this symbol were usually made from red stones such as carnelian and jasper, or from red glass.

The *djet* and the *tit* – represented here again and again united – can be understood as the final marriage of the male and the female principle. This alludes to the *essence of Pharaonic thinking*: It is the striving for the repeated attaining of this *two-oneness* as the aim of the process of renewal and rejuvenation of life: May the corpse of the deceased king enter into the womb of his mother Isis/Nut, and, with her help, turn into Osiris-Tutankhamun; and then, with the help of the knowledge for the afterlife, enter into the eternal circular movement of his father, the Sungod *Re*, thus becoming a two-oneness, *Osiris-Re*.

As the final goal of resurrection of Osiris-Tutankhamun is the unification of his corpse with the celestial spirit, a unification of matter and spirit, we can also understand this conjunction as being represented by this outer decoration of Shrine I, with its repeated union of the male and female principle.

In various Theban tombs of the nobles, a similar decoration of this repeated unification of *djet*-pillar and *tit*-knot can be found on the shrine that contains the mummy. Thus the decoration of the tomb of Tutankhamun shows in various places the ongoing influence of the Amarna period, where the style of royalty came to resemble more closely the style of non-royal tombs.

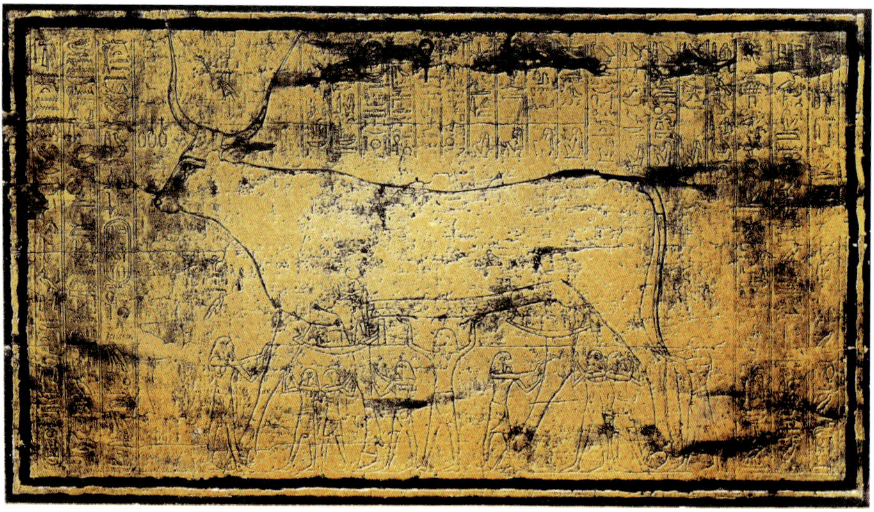

Fig. 102: Golden heavenly cow inside Shrine I, published by A. Piankoff.

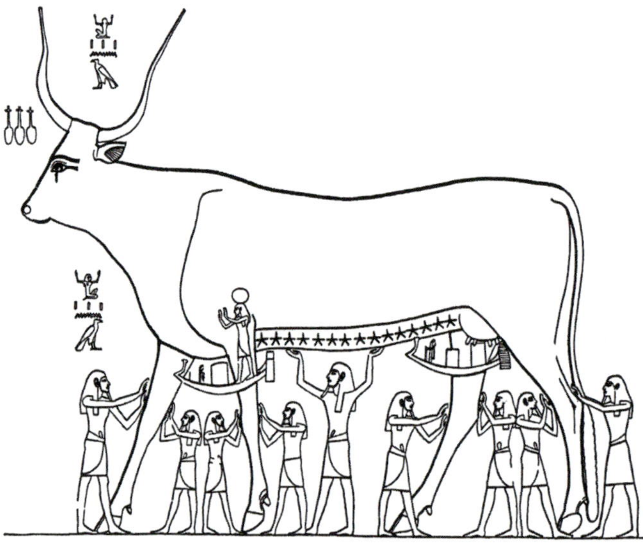

Fig. 103: Divine heavenly cow, diagram of the representation in the picture above.

16b. Shrine I, inside

In Shrine I we find the earliest known copy of *The Book of the Heavenly Cow.* It represents the culmination of the transformation of the dead king to his resurrection as *Re-Osiris*.

It is the divine cow, named *The Great Swimmer* (*Mehet-weret*) that we already met inside Shrine IV (p. 103). She collected the Sungod in the primeval water *Nun* and carried him out of the water on her back or between her horns, thus giving birth to him. This is, of course, a paradox because at the same time the Sungod is said to have created himself by himself.

As the body of the deceased king, as Osiris-Tutankhamun, also dissolves in the primeval water *Nun*, it will again be the celestial cow that will collect him and will carry him to resurrect out of the *Nun*. She transports him through the cosmic night to bring him over the horizon as rejuvenated *Re-Osiris* in the morning.

The following text is unique, not to be found in any later version of this book written about the cow: «*Come, my earthly son, whom I love, king Neb-kheperu-re (Tutankhamun), in order that you will remain together with your father as one of these gods, who are in his retinue, at the side of Meret-weret!*»

This text shows that the divine cow is now going to deliver the resurrected Pharaoh, so that he may stay forever as one of the gods in the retinue of his father, the Sungod Re, becoming thus *Re-Osiris.*

This journey to the resurrection of Osiris-Tutankhamun is taking place at the same time in the barque of the Sungod, which can be seen twice in this representation, inside Shrine I (fig. 103). In all versions of *The Book of the Heavenly Cow*, the direction in which this barque sails is from left to right, from the head of the cow to its back. This means that the barque moves from the West (the mouth), the place of the sunset, through the body of the celestial cow to the back of the cow, to the East, as place of sunrise, where she gives birth to the resurrected *Re-Osiris* (fig. 104).

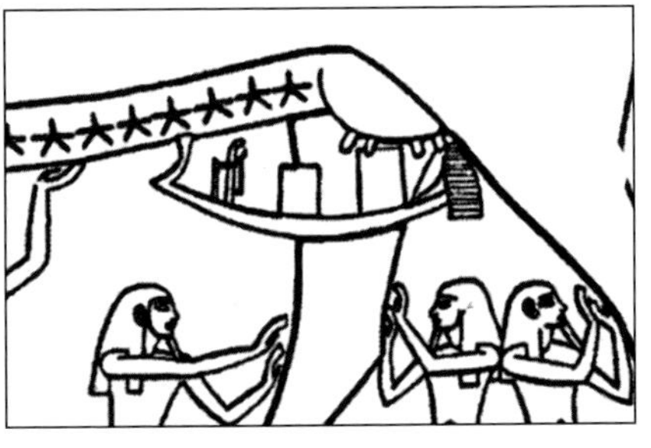

Fig. 104: Barque of the Sungod arriving at the back of the cow, ready to be reborn.

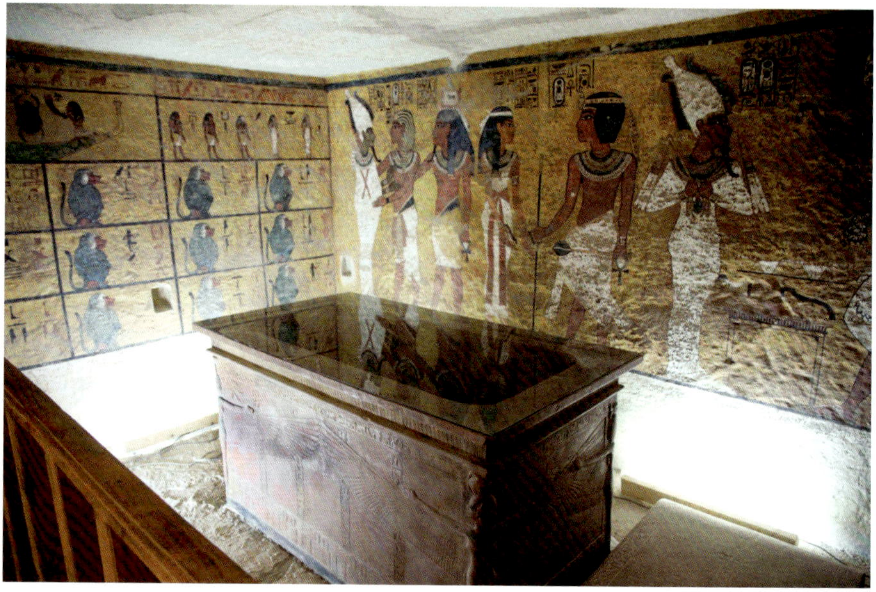

Fig. 105: The quartzite sarcophagus in the original tomb.

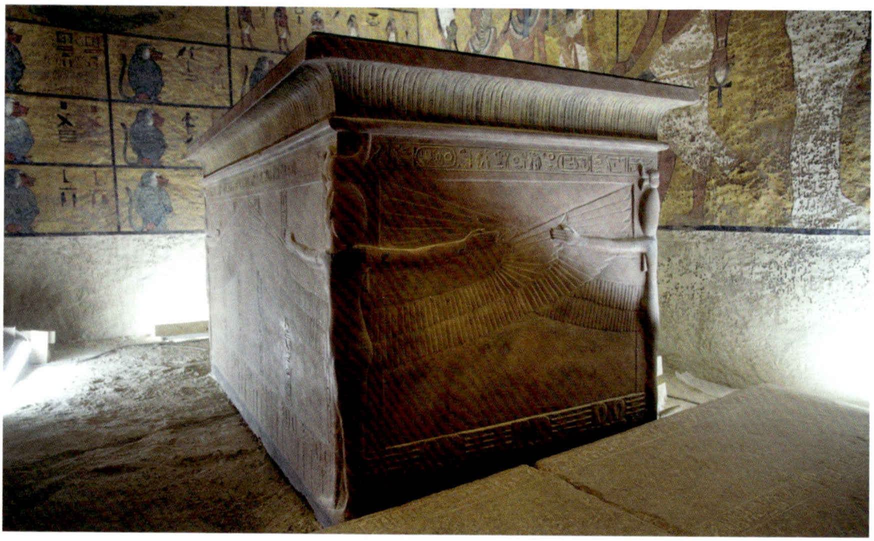

Fig. 106: The facsimile of the quartzite sarcophagus.

17. The quartzite Sarcophagus

Well protected by the four gilded shrines, the discovery of the sarcophagus was a further highlight for Howard Carter. He made a careful drawing of the location of the sarcophagus (fig. 77, p. 97).

Factum Arte was able to recreate in stone the reddish quartzite sarcophagus which can be seen in the facsimile tomb (fig. 106, 107).

In the four corners, four goddesses protect this reddish sarcophagus. In front of the visitor, on the right, we see *Nephthys* and on the left, *Selkis*. The goddesses on the back are *Isis* to the right and *Neith* to the left. These four goddesses were all understood as being different aspects of Tutankhamun's divine mother, the sky-goddess Nut. These deities are worked in high relief, protecting the deceased king with their outspread winged arms (fig. 105, 106).

Unlike the sarcophagus of his father Akhenaton, who placed his wife Nefertiti on all four corners to protect his mummy, the sarcophagus of Tutankhamun again has the traditional four goddesses *Isis, Nephthys, Selkis* and *Neith* to protect the corners of his sarcophagus.

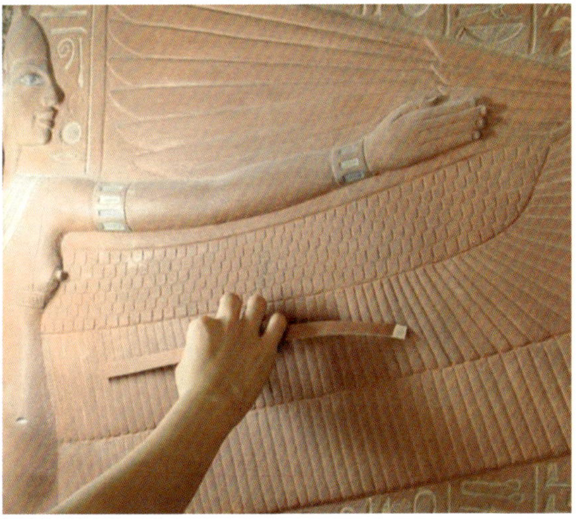

Fig. 107: Work on the facsimile of the sarcophagus: colour check.

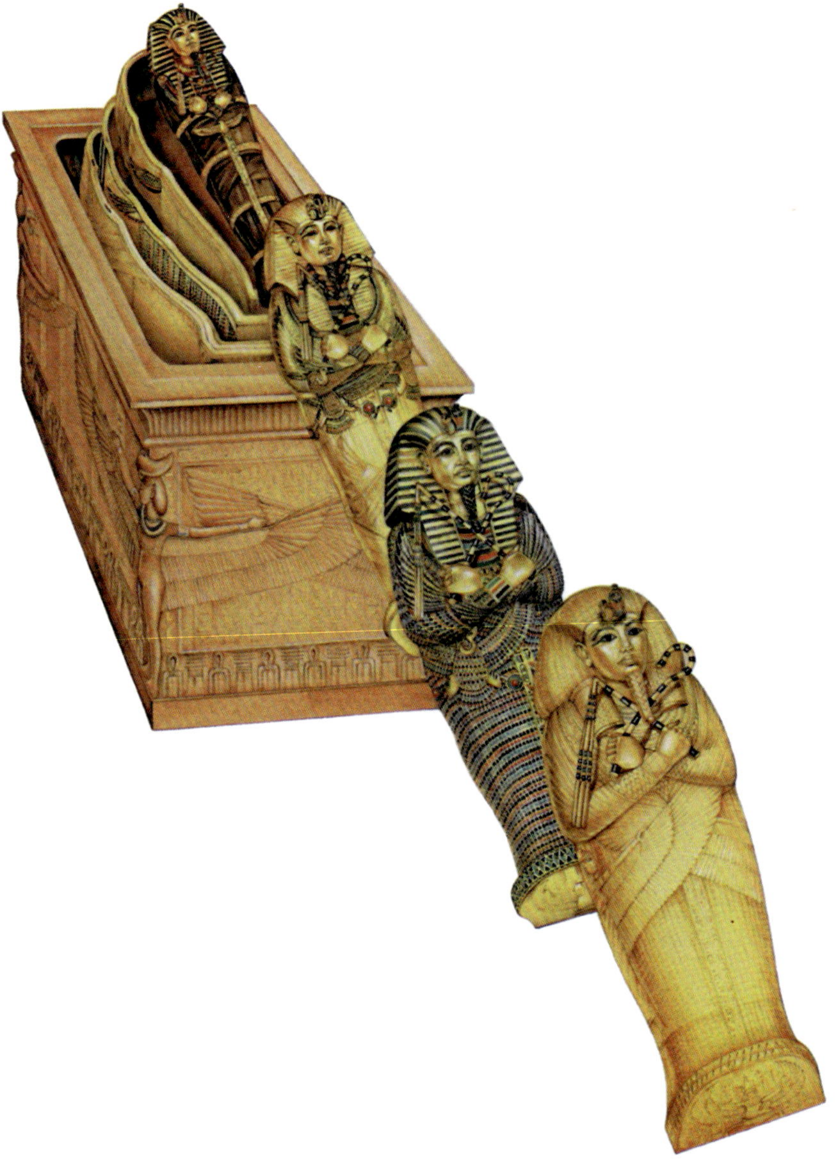

Fig. 108: Inside this sarcophagus were inserted three gilded anthropomorphic coffins. The last of them contained the mummy with its famous golden mask. A flower was found on the mummy, may be placed there from his widow.

18. The three Coffins inside the Sarcophagus

Inside this quartzite sarcophagus, three coffins were placed (fig. 108). These three coffins, with the last one containing the mummy, were made in the traditional form of the god *Osiris*, for, at the time of death, a deceased person was turned – by the mummification process – into Osiris-NN (NN standing for the name of the deceased). By the process of transformation described earlier, the dead Osiris-Tutankhamun was then gradually identified with his father, the Sungod Re, whose main symbol was the metal gold. The outer two of the Osiris-shaped coffins are gilded, while the third innermost one, which contained the mummy, was made of pure gold. On the mummy of Tutankhamun we can see (in fig. 108) the famous solid gold mask (see also next page).

The two inner coffins are now on display in the Egyptian Museum in Cairo, while the outermost third coffin remained inside the original tomb of Tutankhamun. Looking at all the protecting covers for the mummy of the deceased king – shrines, stone sarcophagus and coffins – we can see what enormous effort was made to protect and support the gradual transformation of the individual Osiris-Tutankhamun, in order that he might become ready to unite with his father, the Sungod Re. This placing of so many illustrated layers of protective covers around the mummy shows that, in accordance with the beliefs of the ancient Egyptians, the process of becoming *Re-Osiris*, this two-oneness of matter and spirit, of Osiris-Tutankhamun and the Sungod Re, was considered to be a process for which the deceased had to have the necessary knowledge, in order to avoid the perils of the Netherworld. This gradual, subtle deification, carried out with utmost care, was projected onto the afterlife in Pharaonic times.

Today, this process has become an important task for the individual, namely to reunite the inner opposites and to become conscious of this inner greater human being, albeit *without* identifying with this divine centre. This is a task that is in line with the Pharaonic culture, and remains an ongoing challenge for mankind.

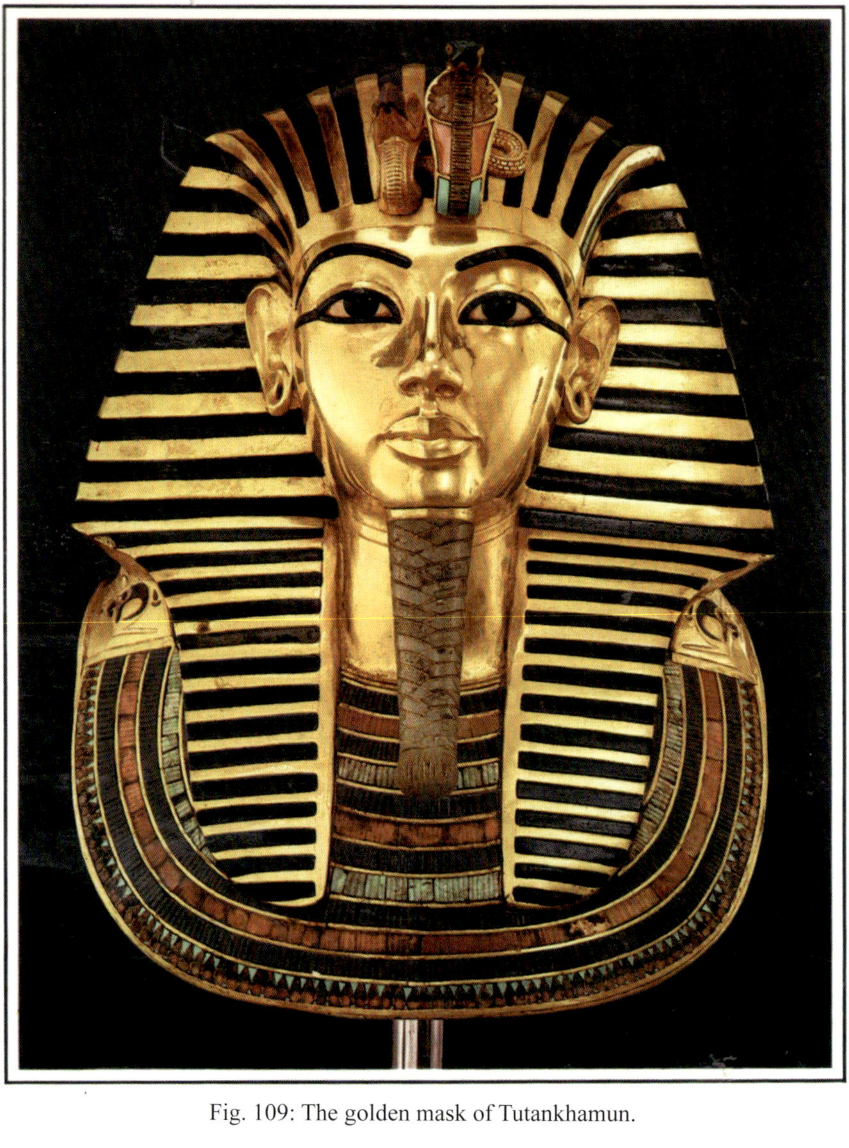

Fig. 109: The golden mask of Tutankhamun.

19. The golden funerary Mask

A magnificent, most impressive mask, made of solid gold, with stripes of blue glas in imitation of *lapis lazuli* on the hairdress protected the head and the upper chest of Tutankhamun's mummy. Tutankhamun's death mask represents the deified Pharaoh, who joined the golden Sungod Re. For the deceased Pharaoh and for his people, this ensures a solar, i.e. eternal, afterlife. This world-famous gold mask is today displayed in the Egyptian Museum in Cairo, together with many other artefacts from the tomb.

The idealised golden face with its eyes, made of quartz and obsidian, gazes at the visitor, expressing rejection of all superficial aspects of life. In so doing, in a mysterious way it revives – in not a few human beings – fundamental questions with regard to the eternal aspects of their own lives. It is as if this mask, created by an outstanding craftsman some 3,300 years ago, were a symbol of our own inner self, looking at us, asking: *Now, and what about you? Are you going to become aware that you have such an inner greater self within your psyche, as well?*

The quest for immortality, as it becomes visible in the tomb of Tutankhamun, and in the accompanying text and images, could thus become a source of inspiration for visitors to the tomb of Tutankhamun.

The 1:1 facsimile of this tomb now allows the visitor to stay in the tomb for a while and thus ponder on the meaning of its discovery many hundreds of years after it was constructed. How and why was this tomb discovered by a dedicated archaeologist precisely *in our time*, its whereabouts having been unknown for so long? In the facsimile tomb, a visitor can reflect on the sequence of pictures and the quest for immortality, without feeling that his or her visit could be contributing to the gradual destruction of this tomb.

Let us now, at the end of our tour, remember that with every breath, a visitor exhales bacteria, mould, and moisture. With the combination of body heat from crowds of visitors, the climate inside such a tomb can become almost tropical. That is why the only sustainable way of protecting these unique Royal tombs of Egypt will be by the creation of facsimiles, such as this pioneering example of the tomb of Tutankhamun.

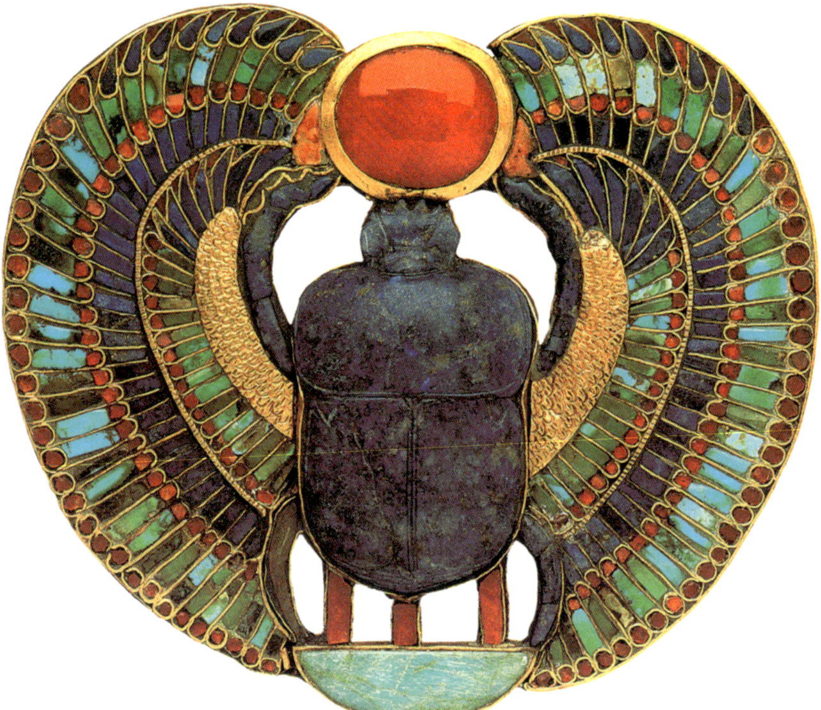

Fig. 110: Scarab, symbol for rejuvenation, carrying the sun-disc. At the same time this image (i.e.: scarab, sun, three stripes connecting to the partial circle, below) represents hieroglyphs that read *Neb-cheperu-re* (Master of manifestations of Re), the throne name of Tutankhamun. The Egyptian Museum, Cairo JE 61886.

Part IV:

Appendix

1. Chronology of the Pharaohs of the New Kingdom

The most important reigns of Pharaohs of the New Kingdom (the years are *Before the Common Era* and are to be understood as approximation).

18th Dynasty	*1540-1292*
Amenhotep I	1515-1494
Tuthmosis I	1494-1482
Hatshepsut	1479-1457
Tuthmosis III	1479-1425
Amenhotep II	1427-1401
Amenhotep III	1391-1353
Amenhotep IV (Akhenaton)	1353-1336
Tutankhamun	1332-1323
Ay	1323-1319
Horemheb	1319-1292
19th Dynasty	*1292-1188*
Ramesses I	1292-1291
Seti I	1291-1279
Ramesses II	1279-1213

Merenptah	1213-1203
Seti II	1203-1196
Tawoseret	1190-1188
20th Dynasty	*1188-1075*
Ramesses III	1186-1155
Ramesses IV	1155-1148
Ramesses VI	1143-1136
Ramesses IX	1127-1108
Ramesses XI	1104-1075

2. Selected Bibliography

Abt, Theodor, “Epilogue” in: Hornung, Erik; Bryan, Betsy (eds.): *Catalogue to the Exhibition “Quest for Immortality. Treasures of Ancient Egypt”*. New York 1999/2000, p. 244-246.

– *Picture Interpretation, According to C. G. Jung*. Zurich 2005.

– *Reviving Egypt's Past for the Future.* Brochure by the Society of Friends of the Royal Tombs of Egypt, Zurich 2009.

Abt, Theodor; Hornung, Erik: *Knowledge for the Afterlife. The Egyptian Amduat. A Quest for Immortality.* Living Human Heritage, Zurich 2003.

Carter, Howard: *The tomb of Tut-Ankh-Amen. Discovered by the Late Earl of Carnarvon and Howard Carter. 3 vols. London 1923, 1927 and 1933.*

Collins, Paul; McNamara, Liam: *Discovering Tutankhamun*. Catalogue to the exhibition, Ashmolean Museum, Oxford 2014.

Darnell, John Coleman: *The enigmatic Netherworld Books of the Solar-Osirian Unity. Cryptographic Composition in the tombs of Tutankhamun, Ramesses VI and Ramesses IX*, Fribourg 2004.

Eaton-Krauss, Marianne: “Tutankhamun”. In: *The Oxford Encyclopedia of Ancient Egypt. Vol. III,* edited by D. B. Redford. Cairo 2001, p. 452-453.

Edwards, Iorwerth E. S.; Burton, Harry; Boltin, Lee: *Tutankhamun. His Tomb and its Treasures*. Cairo and New York 1978.

Fabianis, Valeria Manferto de; Accomazzo, Laura (eds.): *Tutanchamun. Der ewige Glanz des jungen Pharaohs*, Text by T. G. Harry James, photographs by Araldo de Luca, Köln 2000.

Factum Arte: *Factum Artes Work in the Tombs of Tutankhamun, Nefertari and Seti I. March - May 2009,* Project Report, Madrid 2009.

Factum Arte: *Press release selection on conservation projects 2003-2008*, Madrid 2010.

Factum Foundation for Digital Technology in Conservation and Factum Arte: *Press Release, 22nd April 2014.*

Hawass, Zahi; Vannini, Sandro: *King Tuthankhamun. The treasures of the tomb.* Thames and Hudson 2007.

– *The Royal Tombs of Egpyt. The Art of Thebes Revealed.* Cairo 2006.

Hornung, Erik: *Conceptions of God in Ancient Egypt. The One and the Many.* Translated by John Baines. London 1982.

– D*er ägyptische Mythos von der Himmelskuh. Eine Ätiologie des Unvollkommenen*. Fribourg and Göttingen 1982.

– *Die Nachtfahrt der Sonne. Eine altägyptische Beschreibung des Jenseits.* Zurich and Munich, 1991.

– "Die Tragweite der Bilder". In: *Eranos Jahrbuch* Vol. 48 (1979), Ascona, p. 183-237.

– *Tal der Könige. Die Ruhestätte der Pharaonen.* Zurich, Munich 1982.

– "Zu den Schlussszenen der Unterweltsbücher", in: *Mitteilungen des Deutschen Archäologischen Instituts Abteilung Kairo*, Band 37 (1981), Festschrift für Labib Habachi, p. 217-226.

Hornung, Erik; Bryan, Betsy: *Catalogue to the Exhibition "Quest for Immortality. The Hidden Treasures of Ancient Egypt"*. New York 1999/2000.

Hornung, Erik; Staehelin, Elisabeth (eds.): *Sethos – ein Pharaonengrab.* Basel 1991.

James, Thomas G. H.: *Howard Carter. The Path to Tutankhamun,* Cairo 1992, 2001.

Leblanc, Christian; Siliotti, Alberto: *Nefertari. Ausgrabungen im Tal der Königinnen.* Augsburg 1988.

Lowe, Adam: *The Authorized Facsimile of the Burial Chamber of Tutankhamun. With Sarcophagus, Sarcophagus Lid and the Missing Fragment from the*

South Wall. 1922 to 2012. The 90th Anniversary of the discovery of the Tomb. Orbis Biblicus et Orientalis, Madrid 2012.

Mastronardi, Philippe: *Verfassungslehre. Allgemeines Staatsrecht als Lehre vom guten und gerechten Staat.* Stuttgart, Wien 2007.

Piankoff, Alexandre: *Les Chapelles de Tout-Ankh-Amon,* Mémoires publiés par les membres de l'Institut Français d'Archéologie orientale du Caire, Fasc. Premier Le Caire, 1952, Fasc. Deuxième Le Caire 1951.

– *The Shrines of Tut-Ankh-Amon. Texts translated with Introduction by A. Piankoff.* Edited by N. Rambova, New York 1955.

Reeves, Carl Nicholas; Wilkinson, Richard H.: *The complete Tutankhamun. The King. The Tomb. The Royal treasure.* Cairo and London 1997.

– *The complete Valley of the Kings. Tombs and Treasures of Egypt's greatest Pharaohs*. Cairo and London 1996.

Romer, John; Romer, Elizabeth: *The Rape of Tutankhamun*. London 1993.

Schulz, Regine; Seidel, Matthias (eds.): *Ägypten. Die Welt der Pharaonen.* Hildesheim Without Year.

Seipel, Wilfried: *Ägypten. Götter, Gräber und die Kunst. 4000 Jahre Jenseitsglaube. Das Grab des Sennefer.* (Catalogue to an exhibition) Linz, 1989.

Society of Friends of the Royal Tombs of Egypt: *Brochure of the Society of Friends of the Royal Tombs of Egypt.* Zurich 2009.

– *Proposal for the Rebuilding of the Royal Tombs of Thebes*. Zurich 1990.

Weeks, Kent R. (ed.); De Luca, Araldo: *Valley of the Kings: The Tombs and the Funerary Temples of Thebes West*, New York 2001.

Wiese, André; Jacquat, Christiane: *Blumenreich. Wiedergeburt in Pharaonengräbern.* Catalogue to the Exhibition at Antikenmuseum Basel and Sammlung Ludwig, Basel 2014.

3. List of Illustrations

4. Glossary

Akh: An ideal state of being of a deceased, who continues to live. A state, which every blessed, justified deceased can reach.

Amduat: Egyptian book of the Netherworld. Literally meaning: «What is in the Dat (Underworld)». It is describing the journey of the dead Pharaoh following the Sungod Re on his night-journey of renewal through the Netherworld.

Ankh-sign: Egyptian sign for life.

Amun: «The Hidden One» chief deity of the New Kingdom, as Amun-Re associated with the Sungod.

Anubis: A canine-headed god of the embalming process. He preserves the dead from decay and assists and guides those in the transitional realm between life and death in the Netherworld, guiding them on their journey of renewal.

Atef-crown: White crown with two ostrich-feathers on each side. Osiris wears the Atef crown as a symbol of the ruler of the underworld.

Aton: Egyptian word for the sun-disc during the day. The one and only god for Akhenaton, who was probably the father of Tutankhamun.

Ba: The common Egyptian word for soul, capable of leaving the body and moving freely up to heaven. The Sungod Re was seen as the Ba of Osiris.

Carter house: House in the Valley of the Kings, where Howard Carter stayed during his excavation works.

Day-barque: Barque of the day, in which the Pharaoh travels over the sky.

Hathor: Goddess representing all aspects of regeneration, guide of the Sungod in the Netherworld.

Horus: Ancient god of the sky, as falcon or falcon-headed, also seen as son of Osiris and manifestation of the Sungod.

Isis: Sister-wife of Osiris, who brings him back to life after he was murdered by his brother Seth. Later she became the universal female principle.

Ka: Inherent capacity to life possessed by every living creature. Male generative power and life giving principle in gods and humans, also a nutritive force, that is continually sustaining and preserving the body through life as well as in afterlife. As hieroglyph Ka is depicted with two uprised arms.

Ma'at: The right order of the world, justice and truth, personified as a goddess.

Mehet-weret: Celestial cow, literally: «the great flood».

Neb-kheperu-re: Throne name of Tutankhamun. See in glossary under "throne name".

Nefertem: Son of Sekhmet, born out of a lotus flower symbol for the renewed Sungod.

Nehes: Divinity that is part of the crew in the barque of the night, accompanying the Sungod on his journey to renewal.

Neith: Female deity, protecting the dead corpse and ensuring its recreation. Daughter of Nun and Mehet-Weret, associated to primeval time and daily recreation.

Nemes: Striped head-cloth worn by Pharaohs. It covered the whole head and had two large flaps which hung down behind the ears and in front of both shoulders.

Nephthys: Goddess and sister of Isis, sister of Osiris and sister-wife of Seth; often depicted together with Isis, either mourning Osiris or keeping the sun-disc in motion. Child of the sky-goddess Nut and the earth god Geb.

Netjer: Egyptian word for God (n-t-r).

Night barque: Barque of the night, in which the Pharaoh travels on his nocturnal journey in the Beyond.

Nun: The primeval ocean, surrounding and regenerating the cosmos.

Nut: Sky-goddess, giving also birth to the renewed Sungod.

Ouroboros: Greek word, meaning 'tailbiter', in Egyptian 'Tail in mouth'. Image of a serpent having the tail in its mouth. It became later a central symbol of alchemy.

Osiris: Ruler of the Netherworld. He was murdered by his brother Seth and brought back into life by his sister-wife Isis.

Ram: The nocturnal form of the Sungod; the head of a ram is one of the hieroglyphs for the *Ba*-soul; to be distinguished from many other gods who can appear as a ram, like Amun, Khnoum, or Herychef.

Re (or Ra): The Sungod.

Register: Shows the horizontal sequence of scenes within the hours of the night in the Books of the Underworld (*Amduat, Book of Gates etc.*).

Sed-festival: Sed festivals were jubilees celebrated after a ruler had held the throne for thirty years and after that every three years. The festivals were celebrated to rejuvenate the Pharaoh's strength while still sitting on the throne, strengthening the continued success of the Pharaoh.

Sekhmet: Goddess of war, disease but also of healing. Her statues show a sitting or standing woman with a lion's head. She bears a sun-disc on her head. Her son is Nefertem.

Selkis: Egyptian goddess, depicted with a scorpion on her head. Together with Isis, Neith and Nephthys, she is one of the four protective goddesses that were often depicted on the sarcophagus.

Throne name: A king's throne name is usually assigned at his coronation. In hieroglyphs, it is usually preceded by the title *nsw-bity*, which means «King of Upper and Lower Egypt».

Udjat-eye: Mutilated eye of Horus or the Sungod, which is healed (*udja* means healed) and made complete again. Very popular as an amulet.

Uraeus-serpent: Greek word for the Egyptian name for the upraised cobra as protection, worn by Pharaoh or Gods on the forehead as fire-spitting serpent.

5. Index